Things They *NEVER* Taught You

In

CHORAL METHODS

Things They *NEVER* Taught You In CHORAL METHODS

Nancy Smirl Jorgensen · Catherine Pfeiler

With Foreword by Eph Ehly

HAL•LEONARD™ CORPORATION

7777 WEST BLUEMOUND ROAD   P.O. BOX 13819
MILWAUKEE, WI 53213

Printed in the U.S.A.

Library of Congress Cataloging in Publication Data

Jorgensen, Nancy Smirl.
Pfeiler, Catherine.
    Things They Never Taught You In Choral Methods.
        A Choral Director's Handbook.

LCCN 94-73513
ISBN 0-7935-4212-X

TABLE OF CONTENTS

FOREWORD

Two exemplary secondary choral conductors, Nancy Jorgensen and Catherine Pfeiler, in their pursuit of excellence, have presented us with essential things "they never taught us in methods classes."

Their recommendation to "draw the line in the sand" is great advice for conductors who have uncompromising expectations of developing and maintaining a quality choral music program.

Although a must-read for the beginning teacher, these pages contain an abundance of noteworthy suggestions equally important for the experienced teacher/conductor who has shared the same problems but, until this publication, has gone without the solutions. What makes this text such a good read is that the authors have capsulized their ideas and experiences in an up-to-date clever language which will provide the reader with a healthy vocabulary that's easy to incorporate into any existing methodology. Each chapter concludes with some "Practical Suggestions" which serve as handy daily guides along with numerous forms, posters and letters.

Armed with guidelines for selecting quality literature and maintaining standards of religious neutrality in public school, this book goes far beyond the usual prescribed fundamentals of a well constructed secondary methods class curriculum.

For those who wish to "raise the ceiling on their dreams" of developing an outstanding choral program, "Things They Never Taught You In Choral Methods" is a must.

One of many notable quotes effectively placed throughout these pages is, "Success does not come to you - you go to it." Nancy Jorgensen and Catherine Pfeiler have brought some formulas for success to our fingertips so now "you go to it" and you will find a book that is not only informative but remarkably entertaining as well.

Eph Ehly, DMA
Conservatory of Music
University of Missouri - Kansas City

ACKNOWLEDGMENTS

We gratefully acknowledge the influence and inspiration of all the fine choral directors whose work we have studied and attempted to emulate.

Eph Ehly
Douglas McEwen
Allen Wortman
Charlene Archibeque

James Kimmel
Weston Noble
Anthony Baresi
Alverno College Sisters

We also acknowledge with tremendous gratitude the collegial friendships of choral directors with whom we have shared so many years in choral education.

James Vine
Dan Risgaard
Ruth Leithold
Susan McAllister
James Machan
Robin Whitty
Kurt Chalgren
Rick Bjella
Jeanne Julseth-Heinrich
Randy Swiggum

Paul Gulsvig
Karen Luher
Sue Halloway
Ruth Knoll
John Raleigh
Nancy Ehlinger
H. C. Reichold
Blair Bielawski
Sue Cawley
Mark Aamot

We extend a sincere thank you to our state music education organization for their leadership:

Mr. Jack Pingel
Mr. Michael George

We recognize our families for their interest and support:

Shirley, Mary and Nancy Pfeiler
Dorothy and Quentin Smirl, Steven Smirl and Susan Erickson
Joel, Elizabeth and Gwen Jorgensen

We thank those who have made special contributions to our lives:

Michael L. Markson
George Johnston

We acknowledge our administrators and colleagues at Arrowhead High School and thank especially our superintendent, Mr. Dave Lodes, and our mentor, Mr. James Martin, whose idea it was for us to embark on this project. We acknowledge and thank all of our students and parents who make our work enjoyable and worthwhile. We thank the Hal Leonard Music Corporation and especially Janet Klevberg, Choral Editor.

Our endeavor would have been only a dream had not Emily Crocker, editor, composer and clinician, seen value in our project and put her faith in us.

INTRODUCTION: In Pursuit Of Excellence

Excellence. Excellence and its pursuit. It cannot be said too often or stated too strongly that those searching for the key to success in choral music must set aim on this goal. Too often we see the latest warm-up, a clever approach to recruiting or the catchy, new song as the key to our success. Useful as all of these may be to the outcome, success will be assured only if excellence is the clearly established goal.

> *"Excellence is never an accident; it is always the result of high intention, sincere effort, intelligent direction and skillful execution; it represents the wise choice of many alternatives."*

A quality choral program has as its cornerstone the complete dedication to excellence and accepts no substitutes. For ten years we have taught as a team, single-mindedly on course toward a goal of excellence and professionalism. We've allowed ourselves to be influenced by great men and women in choral music and have adopted Eph Ehly's motto of "NO MORE COMPROMISES" as our own. Our intent is to provide a handbook on choral music that goes beyond readily available information on vocal exercises, public relations and conducting techniques. Our goal is to set a practical course for choral directors in pursuit of excellence.

CHAPTER ONE

OWNERSHIP
The Decision to Buy or Lease

Those of us who love choral music and set out to be choral directors embark on a wonderful adventure. Those just beginning the journey might be dismayed to know that the musical approach one adopts has little to do with a group's success. Excellence is neither guaranteed nor determined by the choral school of thought to which one subscribes. The secret of a great choir has little to do with the prestige of the college from which one graduates. Knowledge of musical style, conducting expertise and personal magnetism aside, the work we do is about people.

> *Coming together is a beginning;*
> *Keeping together is progress;*
> *Working together is success.*

Before we decide Bach or Berlioz, before we discuss dynamics and diction, we must give serious thought to these people, our singers, our choir. How can we bring them together, united in the search for excellence in choral singing?

SHARING THE LOAD

One of the ways to share the load is to share the ownership. When singers are part owner in their choir, they will work harder and care more deeply. The director's responsibility is to show students how ownership will be shared. Each choir member should feel that they belong to the choir and that the choir belongs to them. Making students responsible for this possession, for its care and nurturing, is part of the pride of ownership.

THERE ARE NO SMALL PARTS

A few years ago, loading the equipment truck for out of town trips was one of the most frustrating aspects of our travel, especially when an excessive number of ladders, stools, platforms, boxes and other props needed to be transported. The director had assumed responsibility for seeing that everything was packed safely, and nothing was left behind. (In reality a few strong individuals were usually coerced into wrangling the equipment onto the panel truck!) Could the idea of ownership be applied to heavy lifting? Optimistic that the idea would work, we elevated two males, who happened to be of the well-respected, macho variety, to the exalted position of "TRUCK CREW." In the presence of the entire choir, they were told with great bravado that theirs was one of the most important responsibilities on the team.

> "Great discoveries and achievement invariably involve the cooperation of many minds."
>
> "Teamwork is a true challenge. It means coordinating our efforts with those of others - not solely for personal glory, but for team achievement."
> —Unknown

They were reminded of the reputation they must uphold based on the outstanding work of last year's crew. Bolstered by our confidence in them, they assumed OWNERSHIP and did a commendable job. "TRUCK CREW" has since become a position of respect and admiration. Responsibility brought on by ownership developed this position into a true model of excellence, an essential for success.

Ownership requires that every task performed in the choral experience become special. Equal praise should accompany every task, be it singing second soprano, accompanying or loading and unloading the truck. An equal sense of responsibility and pride comes from an equal amount of praise and appreciation.

COMPANY OWNERSHIP

In the pursuit of excellence, everyone shares and cares about the same goals. It should be "our" choir, not "my" choir, and "we," not "me." A director who values singer ownership will be a good listener, asking for others' opinions. It must be clear to each member that he/she is a person of worth, and not merely another voice in the section. It is not necessary to vote on every issue, but when individual likes and dislikes are recognized, singers are more likely to find an investment in choir worth the time and effort. In spite of our efforts toward ownership, there may still be a few who decide merely to lease for a year, but the goal is for every member to feel

> "The team player knows that it doesn't matter who gets the credit as long as the job gets done."

a sense of pride and ownership in the choir. Ultimately, the real magic lies in the feeling experienced when the music and all it has to offer is what truly matters.

SOME PRACTICAL SUGGESTIONS:

1. Observe the three C's: *Consult, Collaborate, Credit.* Consult often with students to encourage a feeling of ownership. Involve them in the planning process. Encourage ideas. Collaborate with them and share the credit that accompanies success.

2. Observe the three D's: *Demonstrate, Delegate, Decorate.* Demonstrate the correct way of doing things, then delegate projects to students thereby encouraging leadership and ownership. Select students to serve as section leaders. Expect them to take honest and accurate attendance and to be efficient with choir housekeeping tasks. Decorate, praising their efforts.

3. Encourage group identity. Design group T-shirts, buttons, and hats.

4. Make a recording for profit or as a wonderful memento.

5. Photograph the group frequently in formal and informal shots. Maintain a scrapbook of choir activities. Singers love the extra attention these items give as ownership and pride in the group increases.

6. Draw attention to those who participate in special events. (e.g., our Solo-Ensemble participants were dubbed the "Magnificent 70" to give extra status to their work.)

7. Make Friday a "Quartet Day." Each person needs to feel accountable for the music and important as an individual with talent in the group effort. This is particularly important in larger ensembles. Have students evaluate one another, allowing those who lack individual vocal ability the opportunity to show musical knowledge through critical listening and student assessment.

8. Avoid using the concert as a lectern for the director to present a running commentary. When a short spoken introduction to a song is appropriate, allow singers to deliver it. Take this opportunity to teach poise and grace in public speaking.

9. Empower students. In sectional rehearsals, assign talented student musicians to review parts. In a choreography session, students can practice playing the role of teacher.

When singers develop a sense of ownership, they are more likely to make an investment that is evidenced through hard work, commitment, and loyalty. They decide to buy into the organization rather than merely lease a chair for a year. The willingness of directors to share the work, and the credit as well, serves as preventive medicine to the egotism that may stand in the way of excellence. A wise person recognizes that the work of developing and maintaining a choral ensemble is too important not to be shared.

CHAPTER TWO

NO MORE COMPROMISES

The Line in the Sand

It was a cold, dreary October morning when the authors met Dr. Eph Ehly for the first time. Tired and a bit overwhelmed from the year's frantic beginning, we wondered why we had given up a free day to attend music convention when shopping would have been more fun. What we heard at convention that day made an important difference to our program. It gave us hope and courage and strengthened our resolve. The words that Eph Ehly spoke have become the cornerstone of our choral program. He admonished us to accept NO MORE COMPROMISES. He urged us to draw our line in the sand and to never allow erosion from our values and ideals. Dr. Ehly is a realist. He knows the kind of battle a choral director wages in delivering a quality program, and the obstacles placed in the path of that ideal. He also believes it is possible to maintain one's principles even in the face of tremendous opposition.

> *Success and achievement seem to happen regularly to people who focus on a goal, even when that goal appears to be impossible.*

QUALITY SELLS ITSELF

After a changing of the guard a few years ago, the authors began teaching in a high school where the tradition of pop music was well established. With a little coercion, much flattery and a great deal of hard work, the students were persuaded to sing a difficult French madrigal, a challenging black spiritual, and additional pieces of quality choral literature. Their achievement was given the praise it deserved, but the real success was that the resultant musical experiences were reward enough for the students. Singer pride increased proportionately with their accomplishments and they became enamored with their sound, the emotions experienced and the challenges met. Later in the year, when we placed a top 40 chart in their folders, they were insulted to think that we would ask them to sing "that easy song." We had unwittingly created musical elitists!

In an effort to present challenging literature, and to refuse to compromise on high expectations, we won the students' commitment to this new concept. In so many battles, the uncompromising ideal will win on its own merit. It is the director's responsibility to point students toward high performance standards and quality music. The "NO COMPROMISE" experience offered students will sell itself.

BEHAVIORAL EXPECTATIONS

As conscientious music educators, we should introduce our students to quality music. We should also encourage our students to become sensitive human beings. A model choral program must have at its core certain standards for student behavior, clearly defined and mutually agreed upon. Begin with the basics. Remind students that good manners are always appropriate and should be prominently displayed. Words like "please," "thank you," "good morning," and "good-bye" should be used regularly.

> "Success seems to be largely a matter of hanging on after others have let go."
> —William Feather

Students must be taught to have respect for others' property. A teacher's desk is private property; nothing should be moved or removed from it without permission. Borrowing books and records is a privilege. Students should follow proper check out procedures, take care of them and return them promptly.

Respecting others' ideas is as important as respecting others' property. Students may disagree but may not disregard. Impolite words, off-color remarks and racial slurs must not be tolerated.

Some inexperienced teachers are surprised and offended by certain students' lack of manners. The absence of polite behavior is often interpreted as a lack of respect. This is not always the case. Usually students simply need remedial instruction in civilized behavior. A cursory glance at the state of modern education shows that teachers are asked to assume more and more of the responsibilities that used to be the teaching province of the family. To develop musicianship, and encourage good citizenship and politeness on the part of our young people, we must not compromise on student behavior.

GRADES

There is no place for compromise in grading. Grades are a powerful tool and should be used wisely and fairly. Standards should be set and observed uncompromisingly, allowing grades to reflect the student's achievement accurately. When grades are an accurate assessment of performance, they can affect behavior dramatically.

> "There is often a reason for not being on time – but it is never a good one!"

Begin with a written document detailing classroom expectations. Rehearsals can be assessed points, awarded only for successful rehearsals. Make it clear that merely warming a chair does not justify a good grade or a credit in a quality choral program. Successful completion of a rehearsal demands promptness, hard work, and devoted attention to the music.

NO SECOND CHANCE FOR FIRST IMPRESSIONS

Students should be introduced to the importance of appearance and the manner in which they present themselves in public. First impressions count, and there is no reason to compromise on something that requires only a small effort and little talent. If your school owns robes, insist that they are always pressed. Discuss proper shoes and hose which will complete the clothing ensemble. For concerts and appearances, insist on skirts or dresses for the ladies and jackets and ties for the men. Girls can be encouraged, though not required, to wear makeup just as an actor does on stage. On tour, require students to wear nice sport clothes. Draw comparisons between musical performances and presenting oneself at a college or job interview. Dressing appropriately for choir events is good practice for future musical and non-musical appearances.

> "A smile adds a lot to one's face value."

Some directors may find these expectations to be unusual. Students from other schools, observing the appearance of our singers, sometimes assume that all of our students are wealthy. In reality they are simply rich in the knowledge that appearance makes a difference. No matter how much the girl in torn jeans and unkempt hair protests that a book not be judged by its cover, the book's jacket is the first thing to attract a reader. Whether performing for a choral clinician, a community function, or a home audience, singing is an art form that is at least in part visual, and it is not too much to expect students to look as wonderful as they sound.

SOME PRACTICAL SUGGESTIONS:

1. Establish the priorities that are most important to you. Draw a line in the sand. Don't back down from your ideals.
2. Concentrate on at least one idea at a time. Daily, remind students to greet you as they enter the room. When this has become a good habit, encourage them to say good-bye.
3. When behavior has not been acceptable, refuse special privileges.
4. Give a grade that accurately reflects the student's fulfillment of the director's expectations (with absolutely no provision for compromises). Make grades dependent not on some God-given vocal gift, but rather on successful completion of rehearsals, attendance at concerts, and appropriate concert dress. (See example at the end of this chapter.)

> *"There is no room in the arts for mediocrity."*
> —Karle Erickson

5. Create penalties that affect a student's grade. Make them fair and easily determined.
6. Send a student home when concert attire is not acceptable. This needs to happen only once for a director to be taken seriously. Keep some very ugly ties in a drawer. Young men would sooner not wear them twice!

There will always be battles to wage in the struggle for excellence in our choral programs. We must decide when to give in and when to stand our ground. As music educators, we must introduce our students to quality music and help them become sensitive human beings. If this is to happen, and we are responsible for it, we can accept NO MORE COMPROMISES.

It is better to try and fail . . .
Than to fail to try . . .

Your grade in choir is an earned one. It WILL NOT be based, in
any way, on your ability to sing. Rather it will be based upon
the contribution you make to the success of the group. Also,
please remember that because you will not be tested as you are
in academic classes, your grade will be based on your attitude,
your behavior, your attendance in class and at concerts, and
how hard you are willing to work for the excellence of our
organization. It will not be enough merely to SAY that you are
interested in the group's success; you must demonstrate by your
actions that you are dedicated to that goal.

TO EARN AN "A" IN CHOIR, A STUDENT MUST:

1. Be in attendance at all concerts and performances, unless
   illness or family emergency should prevent attendance.
   The student must notify the director BEFORE the event to
   be excused.

2. Be on time to class, in the assigned seat and ready to sing.

3. Having worked on a daily basis on voice parts, demonstrate
   knowledge of vocal parts and have music committed to
   memory at concert time.

4. Demonstrate by a positive attitude and by disciplined
   behavior that the choir's excellence is of prime importance.

5. Participate in some aspect of solo/ensemble competition
   during the third quarter.

6. Show a willingness to cooperate in every way your talent
   permits.

PLEASE NOTE: Excessive absences, whatever their reason, will
result in a lowered grade. Because we have no homework or
tests, attendance is VERY important. Because talking is disruptive
to our group effort, talking in class will likewise result in the
lowering of the grade.

Sample Choir Grading Sheet

CHOIR GRADE PROCEDURE

FOR EACH STUDENT:

1. Ten points is earned for each rehearsal SUCCESSFULLY COMPLETED!

2. 50 points is earned for each concert in which the student participates.

3. The above points are NOT awarded when a student is absent from a rehearsal or concert.

4. Points may be subtracted from a student's total for inappropriate behavior at a rehearsal or concert, e.g. gum chewing, disruptive behavior, tardiness, etc.

5. Extra points may be earned through written or oral reports, or solo or small group performances.

6. At the end of each quarter, points will be totaled, and the grading scale adopted by the high school will be used.

Sample Choir Grading Procedure

CHORAL MUSIC GOALS

1. We rededicate ourselves to the complete, uncompromising commitment of bringing quality music literature to our singers.

2. Demanding a disciplined, professional approach on a daily basis, whether it be in rehearsal, performance or listening, is our goal again this year. We know that there is a direct link between discipline and the resulting quality.

3. A well-rounded musical experience includes knowledge of music history, musical terminology, ability to sight-read and exposure to listening experiences in a variety of musical genres, styles and historical periods. Our goal is to see that our students become fine singers and culturally literate citizens as well.

4. We accept responsibility for instilling certain values, including manners, in our students. As they grow and mature, we encourage personal responsibility, punctuality, tolerance for others and others' ideas. We prepare them for the world outside of *Arrowhead High School*, teaching them appropriate dress and behavior for the world of work. We see this as a continued goal of our program.

5. We continue to stress a drug free lifestyle for all of our students, mentioning hazardous health decisions and stressing habits which will lead to a healthy, productive, long life.

6. We see as one of our goals the encouragement of each student's strengths and talents. We empower students to develop leadership skills and we care about each of our many students as individuals, not just as singers.

7. We continue to provide many opportunities for personal growth outside the school setting. We offer career counseling, make phone calls and write letters to help our students find their place in the next rung of the education ladder. While in our program we prepare them for special auditions and encourage them to try new musical opportunities and experiences. (e.g. Honors Choir, Special Experience Workshops, Kids From Wisconsin, musical theatre and voice lessons, etc.)

Sample Choir Goal Sheet

Dear Parents:

Your student has been chosen to represent the High School Choral Department at Solo-Ensemble Competition on _____. We are very proud of all the solos and ensembles we have entered and look forward to this special day with pride and anticipation.

Here are a few guidelines for this all-important competition:

1. All students MUST ride the buses to and from the event.

2. Buses depart from _____ at _____ for all morning events and at _____ for all afternoon events. The final buses will return about _____ .

3. Concert dress is required for the day. All young men should wear dress slacks, socks, nice shoes, a dress shirt, tie and sweater or sport jacket. All young ladies should wear an appropriately dressy outfit; a dress or skirt and sweater. Skirts should be below the knee or longer. No pants are acceptable on this day. Hose and dress shoes are required.

4. Parents are invited to attend the competition and may bring cameras and video cameras. There is no admission charge.

5. Let your student know how very proud you are of them for achieving membership in our special ensembles. We look forward to a wonderful day and hope you can be with us.

Sincerely,

Your Directors

Sample Acceptance Letter

CHAPTER THREE

SELECTING LITERATURE FOR PERFORMANCE

The Right Stuff

For every choral director, the single most critical task is the selection of literature. Thoughtful, deliberative planning is essential in choosing appropriate choral music. The Tanglewood Symposium directs us to introduce our students to a wide variety of literature. The declaration holds us responsible for presenting music of all periods, styles and ethnic diversities, and it urges us to teach our students ABOUT the literature. A comprehensive program must certainly be our goal; variety and above all, QUALITY are the keys to success!

> *"The quality of a person's life is in direct proportion to their commitment to excellence, regardless of their chosen field of endeavor."*
> —Vince Lombardi

The literature should:
1. Represent diversity of period, style and composer
2. Be of diverse lengths
3. Be a balance of both sacred and secular
4. Be a balance of serious and less serious
5. Include texts using both foreign languages and English
6. Include ethnic, pop, show, and experimental music
7. Reflect an awareness of voice ranges and the abilities of the group
8. Preserve the composition's inherent value when the piece is an arrangement

Leonard Bernstein implored us to search for truly great works of art. Without quality music, a program will never rise above the ordinary.

> *"The experience of music is a dialogue between the performer and the audience."*
> —"Fame"

QUALITY IS EVERYTHING

Directors should never underestimate what young people can do. Eph Ehly says, "Give a man a song he can sing and he will tire of it quickly." If you have chosen music of dubious quality and negligible difficulty, students will not benefit. It is vital therefore to continually challenge the singer. Young singers who could not sight-sing a piece in September, may perform it well by April. Challenge their abilities because the value in performing a difficult but important piece of literature is in the process. Perhaps, in the beginning, an a

> "Two roads diverged in a wood, and I – I took the one less traveled by,
> And that has made all the difference."
> —Robert Frost
> "The Road Not Taken"

cappella piece will need accompaniment, or a French text may need to be sung in English, or a solo portion sung by the entire section. Given time and perseverance, no concessions may be needed and the reward will be singers who long remember a piece because of its inherent and enduring quality. So many directors take the sure and easy road. Opt for the road less traveled and the journey will end in a more musically satisfying conclusion.

Even when the literature is challenging, a diet of any one style is boring. A sound educational program demands a widely varied repertoire. Chronicle each choir's literature, and insist that each group experience a wide variety of styles. Keep a chart for each ensemble. On the chart, place the title of the piece and the composer. After each selection, determine the following:

> "Don't give in –
> give them everything."
> —Eph Ehly

1. Is the piece sacred or secular?
2. Is the piece in a foreign language and if so, which one?
3. Is the piece accompanied or a cappella?
4. From which historical period of choral literature was the piece extracted?
5. What is the meter of the piece?
6. In what key is it written?
7. Is the tempo fast or slow?
8. Is it homphonic or polyphonic?
9. Are there any other significant factors that warrant special attention – for instance, is it a Hebrew folk song or an American spiritual?

Maintaining this chart assures a record of each piece selected. For each choir, for each concert and then for the entire school year, there will be a record, a chart of the literature performed. Using the chart prevents the possibility of singing too many songs from one period; it forces the director to look for the Romantic piece that is sometimes ignored or the vocal jazz chart that is intimidating because it requires extra research or risk.

In the authors' own program, it is important that the concert choir sing in foreign languages. In a year's time students sing in Latin, French, German, Spanish and, of course, English. Using the chart reminds us to achieve the balance we desire and prevents us from overlooking a meter, a period of history or a particular style. It helps to provide the choir with a varied diet of music literature. At the end of the year, the chart serves as a chronicle of what each choir has sung. It is a useful record of programming, but more importantly, it allows the directors to develop a four year plan. Since most of our high school students sing for four years, it is vital that they be offered an all-encompassing smorgasbord of styles in quality choral literature.

> *"Music of value is a recreation and a re-creation of the imagination."*
> —Eph Ehly

Too often, choral directors program music they have most recently sung. Using pieces sung in college choirs, chorale, or madrigal ensemble is not always a bad idea, but the hunt for quality music must go further. The most important consideration should be whether the music is appropriate for a particular group.

One note: The music publishing industry cares very much about the continued success of choral programs. If choral music declines, so also will sales of music. We are partners in providing literature of high quality. Observe the copyright laws. If budgets are low, share your music library with neighboring schools and ask them to reciprocate. A small budget is not an acceptable excuse for poor literature in our schools.

SACRED MUSIC IN THE PUBLIC SCHOOLS

The controversy concerning religious music in our schools forces some serious thought on the subject. The following position statement from the Wisconsin Music Educators Association is a helpful resource in making decisions related to the use of sacred music.

"It is the position of the Wisconsin Music Educators Association that the study of religious music is a vital and appropriate part of the total music experience in both performing and listening. The omission of sacred music from the repertoire or study of music would present an incorrect and incomplete concept of the comprehensive nature of the art form."

The Wisconsin Music Educators Association examines the constitutional issues and offers these guidelines for music educators:

Constitutional Issues

"The First Amendment does not forbid all mention of religion in the public schools; it prohibits the advancement or inhibition of religion by the state. A second clause in the First Amendment prohibits infringement of religious beliefs. Nor are the public schools required to delete from the curriculum all materials that may offend any religious sensitivity.

The following questions are relevant to the constitutional standards of religious neutrality necessary in the public schools.

1. What is the purpose of the activity? Is the purpose secular in nature; for instance, studying music of a particular composer's style or historical period?
2. What is the primary effect of the activity? Is it the celebration of religion? Does the activity either enhance or inhibit religion? Does it invite confusion of thought or family objections?
3. Does the activity involve an excessive entanglement with a religion or religious group, or between the schools and a religious organization?

Guidelines for Music Educators

Music educators should exercise good judgment in selecting sacred music for study and programming for public performances. During the planning phase of instruction or programming, the following questions should be considered by each teacher in determining if a program is acceptable.

1. Is the music selected on the basis of its musical and educational value rather than its religious context?
2. Are the traditions of different people shared and respected?
3. Is the excessive use of sacred music, religious symbols or scenery, and performance in devotional settings avoided?
4. Is the role of sacred music a neutral one, neither promoting nor inhibiting religious views?
5. Are all local and school policies regarding religious holidays observed?

6. Is there understanding of the various religious beliefs and sensitivities represented by the school-children and parents?"

Because we are citizens of the United States where our constitution promises separation of church and state, we are obligated to protect the rights and sensitivities of all our students. In striving to protect students' rights, however, we must not sacrifice a well-rounded repertoire which, by definition, must include some sacred literature.

VOCAL PERFORMANCE: A VISUAL ART

The art of choral music demands both an aural and a visual performance. Weston Noble reminds us that everything we sing is a drama. Every rehearsal is important, but

> *"Develop a romance with your subject – then share it."*
> —Eph Ehly

eventually rehearsals culminate in a public performance. Unless this performance is in a recording studio or for radio broadcast, students must be performance skilled. If as Eph Ehly says, the need to express is paramount, we must teach singers to be expressive, both musically and visually. They must be actors as well as singers. The audience needs to see as well as hear their commitment to the music.

Dr. Ehly states that each piece of music should be regarded as a dramatic play but urges us to avoid too many sit-coms. Instead he insists that when we sing, we must express "the mind, the heart, the spirit and the body. Dull singing does not express personality. The people who are most successful are those who bring music to life."

> *"The only limits are, as always, those of vision."*
> —James Broughton

As directors we must teach our students the acting skills essential in a live performance. Quality literature performed well demands this commitment.

SOME PRACTICAL SUGGESTIONS:

1. Buy a copy of *An Annotated Inventory of Distinctive Choral Literature.* This book lists octavos, the degree of difficulty, and the distinguishing characteristics of each piece. It is an essential directory of quality choral works.
2. Attend workshops, choral reading sessions and music conventions. Take a notebook and a discerning ear. Choose only what you know to be of good quality.

3. Ask colleagues to recommend their most successful pieces.
4. Evaluate arrangements. When you find quality work by an arranger, continue to search for other pieces by the same arranger.
5. Listen to professional recordings of choral groups. *Chanticleer, The King's Singers, The Turtle Creek Chorale* and many others perform outstanding choral literature, some of which is accessible to the high school choir.
6. Watch videotapes of professional choirs and note the singers' facial expressions and subtle movement.
7. Become acquainted with your favorite music store staff. They are a valuable resource in locating special octavos or editions.
8. Listen to the various demonstration tapes sent by music publishing companies. Be discriminating. Choose a piece because of its educational value, rather than because of its availability.
9. Call the publisher when a piece is out of print. They can either find it or give permission to copy.
10. A diet of any one thing is boring. Perform music from each historical period along with folk songs, spirituals and popular pieces.
11. In choosing literature, decide what information a piece can teach – a culture, a composer, a period, an event. Choose music for the concept or skill that can be learned.
12. Don't reinvent the wheel. Save time by looking at graded lists of literature published by ACDA, state solo and ensemble committees, and other sources.
13. Trust your judgment. Make choices a challenge. Students tire quickly of something that is too easy. Satisfaction is earned through completing a challenging piece.
14. Keep learning. We never know enough. Those who stop learning often stop caring as well.

> *"Raise the ceiling on your dreams! Ask, what difference will I make?"*

Time and energy devoted to providing quality literature can earn unexpected rewards. One day a senior in concert choir approached the piano at the end of rehearsal. "Before the end of the year could we please sing my all-time favorite song from sophomore year?" he begged. "What is it?" we wondered. His unwavering answer was, "*Ubi Caritas.* I love that song." His favorite song was not a pop chart from show choir or a number from "Phantom of the Opera." It was the difficult five part Latin motet by Maurice Durufle that had moved him in his sophomore year and lived in his memory.

Music educators mold the future of popular taste. Quality music speaks for itself and will not need the hard sell. Singers rely on the director to present the best in choral music, and they will never come to know what we neglect to have them experience.

LITERATURE CHART

Title	Composer	Accompanied or a cappella	Language	Sacred or Secular	Historical Period	Meter	Key	Other

Sample Literature Chart

LISTENING PLAN CHART

Title/Composer	Artist	Mixed Choir	Women's Choir	Men's Choir	Solo Voice	Renais-sance	Baroque	Classical	Romantic	Contem-porary	Vocal Jazz	Special Style	Foreign Language

Sample Listening Plan Chart

CHAPTER FOUR

OUT HERE ON MY OWN
What They Missed in Methods Class

When the time comes to face the music, and your very own choir is charging through the choir room door, the truth will hit hard. The truth is that no matter how comprehensive your methods classes were, no matter how fine your choral education and secondary conducting instruction were – the truth is

> *"I knew working in the arts would change my life."*
> —Mikhail Baryshnikov

that there are some gigantic surprises out there in the real world called school! Start by accepting this fact and face reality. This is going to be hard work and you will make some mistakes; if you live to tell about it, you will spend some wonderful years working with young people and music. You will even be paid for it.

DID THEY TELL YOU ...

This work takes an enormous amount of physical, mental and emotional energy. The people who do this work well go home tired at the end of a day. Maybe no one mentioned that a choir director sings,

> *"Nothing happens by itself... It all will come your way, once you understand that you have to make it come your way, by your own exertions."*
> —Ben Stein

sometimes while playing the piano standing up, five or six hours a day – and that during the school musical it's more. Successful teachers pace themselves, guarding their teaching tool – their voice – and taking care of themselves.

It's important to guard against being so worn out that judgment becomes impaired. It is also crucial to pace oneself to avoid being physically exhausted. Dr. Eph Ehly says that most teachers who claim to be burned out have never really been on fire. But he also urges choir directors to do these three things:

1. Avoid spreading yourself too thin.
2. Resolve personal problems so they don't interfere with the music making.
3. Make the music and the singers a priority.

It is also vital in the long haul to find balance between work and a personal life. Often the boundary between the two becomes blurred and the demands of work can overshadow one's personal time. A director must guard personal time but not be afraid to give his all to the job. Teaching is a noble way to spend a working life but it has never been a nine-to-five proposition.

SOME PRACTICAL SUGGESTIONS:
1. Be a well-rounded person. Often music and its logical siblings (theater, etc.) are also a choir director's hobbies. Read the newspaper and cultivate non-musical interests as well.
2. Exercise and adopt a healthy lifestyle. To do one's best under stress-filled circumstances one must stay well, physically and mentally.

> "Not in time, place, or circumstance, but in the man lies success."
> —Charles B. Rouss

AND DID THEY MENTION . . .
Classroom management is a skill seldom discussed in methods class. Preparing for the daily rehearsal, and the myriad of details leading up to that rehearsal, is paramount to success. Only when the daily operations are under control can real music and learning happen.

Before the rehearsal starts, and before the students arrive, much can be done to set the stage for success. The choir room must be a special place where everyone feels welcome and by its atmosphere conveys a sense of pride and excellence. While the choir room should suit the educational needs of the director, it must also be a satisfying place for students to congregate both during class time and on their free time. Make an effort to prepare the choral room, insuring that it is conducive to learning.

Once the stage is set, the props must be assembled. The music folder storage units marketed to choral departments everywhere are very attractive and if used will successfully waste a great deal of rehearsal time. The director who is creative musically can certainly be creative in finding a more efficient way to distribute music. Fifty kids standing around a music storage area makes no sense and begins each rehearsal in chaos. Section leaders can assume the responsibility for folder distribution, or student assistants can set folders on chairs if there is a free hour preceding choir.

With the stage set and the props assembled, it's time for blocking. Most of us teach more than one choir and often multiple choirs rehearse consecutively in the same room. This does not mean the room must remain set up in one rigid manner. Varying the use of risers and chairs allows the director to experiment. Changing the setup of the room each day to accommodate different teaching strategies will also prevent stagnant, predictable rehearsal settings.

Preparations such as these are easily ignored, but they are essential to the mental and emotional preparation of the director and the choir. None of these extra preparations do an ounce of good, of course, unless the director is musically prepared. Having a thorough knowledge of the music, studying the score carefully and garnering background information on the pieces are essential to success in the choral classroom. Prepared for the rehearsal, goals firmly established, and music ready, the rehearsal can begin.

SOME PRACTICAL SUGGESTIONS:

> *"Hold yourself responsible for a higher standard than anybody else expects of you. Never excuse yourself."*
> —Henry Ward Beecher

1. Display plaques, trophies, and pictures of each choir and every musical theater production.
2. Stress tradition and create a "The Way We Were" board with alumni pictures and memories of the previous year's accomplishments.
3. Construct a birthday calendar with every member's special day mentioned.
4. Store folders by section in plastic crates. Assign a section leader to distribute and collect the materials each day.
5. Set chairs in a variety of arrangements. One day everyone may be facing the front of the room, the next they can turn 180 and face the back. For another variation, set up each section in its own circle, or have all sections in the round, facing center. Groups of four or eight can be arranged, forcing singers to perform in mixed quartets.

At the rehearsal (so many songs, so little time), there are so many things to accomplish and so many pitfalls that can impede progress. Though maintaining discipline may be difficult at times, a director with firmly established rules will have a better chance of accomplishing established goals. No matter how tired or worn out one gets, maintaining a commitment to discipline will reap positive rewards. Ninety percent of what goes right or wrong in the classroom is because of the person in charge. The truth is that unless a director has a handle on student discipline, unless an atmosphere for learning is created, the director will never have the chance to create beautiful music or to use the musical skills we all care about so deeply.

"The rewards for those who persevere far exceed the pain that must precede the victory."
—Ted Engstrom

"I have come to a frightening conclusion.

I am the decisive element in the classroom.

It is my personal approach that creates the climate.

It is my daily mood that makes the weather.

As a teacher I possess tremendous power to make a child's life miserable or joyous.

I can be a tool of torture or an instrument of inspiration.

I can humiliate or humor, hurt or heal.

In all situations it is my response that decides whether a crisis will be escalated or de-escalated, a child humanized or de-humanized."
—Haim Ginatt

SOME PRACTICAL SUGGESTIONS:

1. Learn each student's name quickly. If a student thinks he is anonymous, he will accept little responsibility for inappropriate behavior.

2. Handle most discipline problems in private. Say, "Glenda, please see me in the choir office at the end of the period." Never publicly fly off the handle or show undue anger to a student.

3. Don't take inappropriate behavior personally. It usually has little to do with the director. Maintain objectivity, get over it quickly, and find a reason to compliment or comment to Glenda the next day, so she knows you are forgiving and reasonable.

4. Boredom can be the root of behavior problems. Keep things moving. Vary techniques so that your teaching is unpredictable.

5. Reinforce positive behavior with sincere, continuing compliments. "I am so pleased with the fine posture of the bass section today!" rather than "Jim, I have asked you a thousand times to sit up straight! What is your problem?"

6. Be consistent from day to day. Students become confused if the director expects it quiet one day and will accept talking on another day.
7. Talk as little as possible and maintain eye contact as much as possible.
8. Attempt to treat students equally. Be as fair as possible and if otherwise accused, explain yourself and be aware that perceptions are as important as reality.
9. A quality music program depends very much on the personality of the director. Be excited about the music, and be a person worthy of admiration. Singers don't care what you know until they know that you care.

> *"Few things are impossible to achieve with diligence and skill... Great works are performed not by strength, but by perseverance."*
> —Samuel Johnson

10. When having a bad day, or when a personal problem threatens to be overwhelming, warn the singers beforehand that they would be wise to proceed with caution. Don't take personal problems out on students.

In an effort to learn a large repertoire of songs, teaching the notes can sometimes prevent teaching the music. When a director becomes glued to the piano bench, real teaching can be forfeited. When students man the keyboard, or when a cappella singing is required, the director can be free to wander the ranks and become physically closer to the choir. This physical proximity allows the director to listen to individuals, become more an integral part of the group setting, and reinforce discipline.

The pacing of a rehearsal can make or break a choir and a quickly paced rehearsal is the overwhelming choice for most days in the high school choral setting. While the director may revel in an endless dissertation on the history of a piece, students need only a quick take on the historical significance of a song. Endless warm-ups with no stated purpose may serve the director well as his own personal showcase, but students need variety and purpose to make warm-ups a useful part of the rehearsal. Most students who sing in a high school choral program are not as enamored of music as the director. They are there to sing because they find it enjoyable. Endless discourse on the origins of Gregorian chant, endless vocalises to purify the vowel, endless anything will not reach the high school singer. For many of our singers, choir is only one of many things they enjoy. Recognizing this is part of the reality of being out here on your own.

SOME PRACTICAL SUGGESTIONS:
1. Greet singers at the door. Require that all books and materials be left away from the rehearsal area. (The need to reprimand students for doing homework will disappear if they bring only a pencil to the rehearsal setting.)
2. Make good posture, no gum and a quiet atmosphere the requirements for a good grade.
3. Start rehearsal at the bell. A late start on a regular basis encourages students to waste other valuable time. It sends a message that choir is less important than academic classes. By starting on time, we stress that choir is important, and that not one moment can be wasted.
4. Use two, three or four pianos. With each part individually accompanied, more students will be singing at the same time. Since many do not read music well, they will learn by hearing their part and be idle for less of the rehearsal.
5. Rotate standing and sitting. Be unpredictable.
6. Try seating each section in a circle so they hear each other and begin to operate more as a team.
7. Experiment with the choral set. Try setting the piano in the center of the room, with all sections facing in.
8. Make one huge circle single file around the perimeter of the room, first with sections standing together, then in mixed formation to encourage independent singing and student accountability for the music.
9. Incorporate very short music theory and history lessons into rehearsals on a regular basis. Use listening lessons weekly, focusing on music a step beyond what the students can actually perform.
10. Explain the purpose of warm-ups. Vary them, using rounds or known songs.
11. Compliment often. Insist on excellence, but use praise when it is deserved.
12. Put announcements in a different spot each day. Allow students to do announcements on occasion.
13. Feature impromptu octets and quartets often. Students enjoy hearing each other succeed. It's also excellent mental practice for those listening.

14. Be flexible. Be willing to change a lesson plan to accommodate unforeseen circumstances.

OH, BY THE WAY...

(Everything you didn't think you needed to know about choral music, and now are afraid to ask) One of the most overwhelming things about choral work is that it requires expertise in so many areas. It is assumed that choral directors will have conducting skills, knowledge of the human voice, and the ability to function at the keyboard. Directors are usually knowledgeable about choral literature, music history, and vocal range, but are often surprised by the other

> *"Success seems to be connected with action. Successful men keep moving. They make mistakes but they don't quit."*
> —Conrad Hilton

areas of expertise that are required throughout a successful career in choral music. What unravels many well-intentioned choral directors is that much of their time in school choral settings is spent doing things for which some colleges have provided little preparation.

There is a solution to this dilemma: consult and collaborate with specialists. Barbershop singing was an area we found demanding because it had specific requirements for which we had no training. We didn't particularly enjoy the literature and yet we knew that barbershop singing would greatly enhance the listening skills and independent singing skills of our young singers. What to do? We called in the experts and asked a ream of questions, we invited clinicians to spend a day with our singers, and we attended workshops on barbershop harmony, eventually entering competitions to see others. Now, after some years of

> *"Success doesn't come to you - you go to it."*
> —Marva Collins

experimenting, learning new approaches, and spending countless hours in trial and error, we are more capable of participating successfully in this specialized area.

Many choral programs produce a musical and anyone who has ever been part of a successful re-creation of a Broadway musical will remember it as a highlight of their musical experiences. The answer when one lacks experience in this genre (and many do) is to form a team. What may be impossible to do alone can be accomplished successfully through collaboration with the drama department, a local dance instructor and the band or orchestra. Attend workshops and read how-to books to supplement your knowledge base. Again, help is out there.

Madrigal singing, vocal jazz, show choir, and the performance of black spirituals are all areas requiring specialized knowledge of literature, style and performance. Don't waste a minute feeling unprepared. Call in a specialist! Ask questions! Someone else took ten, twenty, maybe thirty years to become an authority. Find out what they know. Observe them. Talk to them.

After years of singing black spirituals, we were lucky enough to meet Robert Ray, a black composer and conductor. He offered specific information that enabled our mostly Caucasian singers to correctly stylize the music of Black America. His helpful hints have been invaluable in further interpretation of this special idiom. The point bears repeating. Help is out there! Don't hesitate to ask for it. Form the habit of consulting and collaborating. Choose an idiom and do it very well but don't try to be great at everything all at once. Real success comes from building on small triumphs one by one.

> "The credit belongs to the man who is actually in the arena; whose face is marred by dust and sweat and blood; who strives valiantly; who errs and comes short again and again; who knows the great enthusiasms, the great devotions and spends himself in a worthy cause."
> —Theodore Roosevelt

Offering students a quality experience in a variety of musical activities is the director's responsibility. Lack of expertise in a particular field should never be a reason to deprive students of an activity. But it certainly takes a great deal of extra time (probably unpaid) and effort (sometimes unappreciated) to provide a well-rounded quality choral experience for your singers. Excellent choral programs are never an accident of fate. They are always the result of going that extra mile. Young people are worth the commitment to excellence. They are worth the extra time.

SOME PRACTICAL SUGGESTIONS:

1. Ask a local college professor to share his expertise with your choir. Most are happy to do this since it is also a great recruiting tool for the college.
2. Read the ads, browse the music stores, and network with colleagues to find printed publications in a field for which you are inadequately prepared.
3. Find a class and make time to take it.

4. Pay a clinician (who may or may not be an educator) to share an area of expertise. There are some great musicians out there who do other things for a living. Find them and use their knowledge and expertise.
5. Enter a festival or competition. Observing others can be one of the best learning tools.
6. Invite a colleague who has developed an area of expertise to do a workshop. If money is tight, offer to return the favor rather than pay a fee.

AND DID THEY EVER MENTION . . .

Out here on your own, sometimes the line between sanity and insanity is a fine one. The competent choral director must be organized. We had been out there for quite a while when necessity finally became the mother of invention. The time had come to plan the annual holiday choral program. Privately we had always called the Christmas concert the "Holiday Holocaust" but publicly we title it something more palatable like "Songs of the Solstice." We wanted our students in all four choirs to sing songs not previously sung at any of the past three holiday concerts. Unfortunately we couldn't remember what had or had not been previously programmed. We searched for the printed programs from previous concerts. Where were they? The box in the garage? The file cabinet in the music library? Could they be in the bottom drawer of the desk? We were on the edge, ready to tear our hair out. Frustration gave way to a fresh resolve. We organized our materials into huge three-ring notebooks, with pockets where pictures and programs could be placed. The school provided us with large filing boxes and after some thoughtful organization everything is now more easily found. It took some long hours to organize these notebooks and filing boxes but over the years it will save many hours of frustrated searching. Many people are surprised and impressed to find that creative, artistic people can also be orderly and organized. We found that it kept us from insanity as well.

> "If there is a way to do it better... find it."
> —Thomas A. Edison

> "The kind of people I look for to fill top management spots are the eager beavers, the mavericks. These are the guys who try to do more than they're expected to do."
> —Lee Iacocca

SOME PRACTICAL SUGGESTIONS:

1. Save concert programs and file them chronologically.
2. Save ideas, quotes, catalogs and materials information. Create a file folder for each category.
3. Keep a yearly scrapbook chronicling a year's achievements.
4. It is impractical to save every piece of music received at reading sessions and conventions. Use your own judgment, and toss what you know you'll never use.
5. Maintain a phone number and address book for professional contacts.

> "If a man has a talent and cannot use it, he has failed. If he has a talent and uses only half of it, he has partly failed. If he has a talent and learns somehow to use the whole of it, he has gloriously succeeded and won a satisfaction few men ever know."
> —Thomas Wolfe

Admitting that one's choral education might be incomplete is sometimes a difficult thing to do. Enjoy the adventure of learning new skills. One can never know enough. The mark of a good teacher is the ability to change. People who have stopped learning usually have stopped caring. Read books on personal excellence. The techniques successful people employ are the same whether in business or education. A choral program of quality is the sum of many parts. The joy of learning new skills to achieve that quality will be its own reward.

CHAPTER FIVE

TRADITION! TRADITION!
What Tevye Can Teach Us

"Without our traditions, our life would be as shaky as a fiddler on the roof." So spoke the Jewish milkman Tevye, in the well-known musical *Fiddler on the Roof.* Tevye found strength and comfort in his traditions. Successful choral programs have special traditions that are cherished by students, parents and patrons. Singers, patrons and the community at large develop expectations and assign value to repeated events. When inheriting a program, it is vital to preserve these existing traditions while simultaneously establishing new ones. Both the old traditions and the new are important in building and sustaining a successful choral program. If excellence is the overall goal, maintaining traditions that enhance and complement that excellence is key.

> *"It's not enough to dream your dreams; you've got to pursue your dreams."*

TRIED AND TRUE

A common tradition in many choral programs involves special songs. A song of friendship sung at the final concert, a patriotic number performed at commencement, or the "Hallelujah Chorus" sung on a holiday program — after a few years these songs are expected and become a part of the tradition. Our freshmen and sophomores learn three or four friendship songs during their first semester with us. They are also taught an assortment of warm-up rounds that are part of our tradition and are used during their four year tenure. These songs are known by all of the high school singers and may or may not be performed publicly. They form a core of numbers common to all. On the bus to an event, or when a special need arises, all singers can perform selected songs together. There is a special birthday round and songs always sung at holiday time. Students rely on this sameness, anticipate it and treasure it. A holiday poem frequently recited at our winter concert expresses this sentiment:

> "So much of the joy of Christmas
> Is the sameness of it all.
> Always the wreath upon the door
> The holly in the hall . . . "

So it is with songs, which embed themselves in the choral tradition. The familiar pieces that are repeated from year to year cultivate a valued sentiment. The sheer sameness of the repetition makes all feel comfortable and at home in the program.

GREAT EXPECTATIONS

Consistently high expectations can establish a tradition all their own. Communities recognize high standards of performance and reward students in a variety of ways, i.e., through audience support, monetary and in-kind donations, or political support.

> "Always bear in mind that your own resolution to succeed is more important than any other one thing."
> —Abraham Lincoln

A well-produced musical can be an example of high quality that creates its own tradition. Our own choral department accepts no compromises in the production of the all-school musical. When patrons arrive at the theater, the audience sees a high school foyer transformed into a showcase for the production much like what might be seen in New York. A ticket booth with bright stage lights heralds the opening of the show. Professional pictures are displayed on easels built by shop classes. The program, an almost exact replica of a professional playbill, is printed courtesy of a local printing company. Audiences appreciate and anticipate this transformation of the school. The students delight in the decorating and revel in the extra attention generated by the display. The point is that this complete dedication to making the musical a professional product can become a tradition. Every show can be sold out because patrons know the past excellence of the productions. Even when the show is a lesser known one, the theater will be filled to capacity because of the tradition of excellence cultivated through repeated successes. The extra effort devoted to making the production first class will be rewarded for years to come. *TRADITION!*

Each director will cultivate distinctive traditions, fashioned from old customs and new ideas. Here are a few traditions that are successful in building a feeling of belonging. They also stand alone as important ideas in their own right:

Nominate seniors to fill positions of leadership. Without regard for their vocal abilities, appoint seniors to positions such as section leaders, dance captains and attendance chairpersons. Seniors can form a leadership corps that will be called upon to lead discussions, run sectional rehearsals, and model correct behaviors. They can run the daily operations of choir, head the truck crew when on tour, and serve as consultants when important decisions are made. They can be empowered to serve as leaders, share responsibility for the group's success and be accountable to the younger members. This experience contributes to the development of self-esteem and pride among choir members. The tradition of sharing leadership with seniors is a powerful and important one.

"Success is the maximum utilization of the ability that you have."
—Zig Ziglar

In the musical *Company*, the characters sing, "It's the little things you do together that make perfect relationships." Though they are speaking about the institution of marriage, it seems equally true in the case of student-teacher relationships. Daily interactions among singers and directors can develop into significant choral traditions. Younger students entering a program hear about these traditions and are eager to be part of them. Early morning hours, before rehearsals begin, offer an opportunity for special interaction. This can be the perfect time for informal discussions about musical or extra-musical ideas. Encourage all singers to join in the gathering. An occasional treat of doughnuts or cookies makes for a relaxed atmosphere, and is incentive for some. Encourage students

"Love is the most important ingredient of success. Without it, your life echoes emptiness. With it, your life vibrates warmth and meaning. The best portions of a good man's life – his little nameless, unremembered acts of kindness and love."
—William Wordsworth

to eat lunch together in the choir room. The informal atmosphere facilitates discussions, and students see each other as friends as well as singers. These traditions can become an important part of the students' routine and they can value and look forward to the personal contact each day.

Some secondary educators may think that only elementary students appreciate rewards such as stickers, but older students love them too. We have a large supply of stick-on stars that are placed on students' shirts on concert day, when they board the bus to a special event, or after a particularly rough week. The star is not awarded for anything particular and means only, "I love you and care about you." Sometimes, when a student is having a bad day, he or she will come to the choir room and ask for a star. It gives us the opportunity to comfort, console, help or encourage. Frequently, students give each other stars, and when words are difficult to find, the star can suffice. Students seventeen and eighteen years old know about the stars, ask for them and give them to each other.

> *"Obstacles will look large or small to you according to whether you are large or small."*
> —Orison Swett Marden

The symbolism of the circle can be used with smaller groups. To emphasize the importance of all to the whole, stand in a circle, the symbol of unity and strength. Join hands and sing friendship songs in the circle. Avoid overusing the idea so that it always has special meaning.

BEWARE OF TAMPERING

Be careful when you attempt to tamper with tradition. Our group is fiercely loyal to the show choir colors and any suggestion of modifying or changing these colors is met by a loud chorus of disapproval. For a number of years, the show choir ladies wore pants as part of their costume and this too developed into a powerful tradition that was difficult to change. Trying to achieve a more feminine look, a skirt was suggested instead. The ladies were completely convinced that pants were a success, and saw no valid reason to consider a change. Only after two years of persuasion were all convinced to try the new idea. Some traditions die hard, and it's important to consider feelings of loyalty and commitment when making a major change.

For many years the choir had sung the "Hallelujah Chorus" at Christmas time. Difficult soprano and tenor ranges make that piece, however beloved, a questionable choice for high school singers. It also consumes a tremendous amount of teaching time. So one year it wasn't taught and it wasn't sung and the complaints about the omission didn't stop until April! Long, serious thought is now given to any decision that involves discarding a tradition, and the choir sings the "Hallelujah Chorus" every year at the holiday concert, in spite of its obvious difficulties. When established traditions are important to singers or an audience, it is important to reinforce expectations and insure that the tradition continues.

THE MARK OF EXCELLENCE

A choral program is more than the sum of its parts. Sometimes a tradition itself is important. More often, a director uses traditions to create a distinctive program. To distinguish a program and make it unique, directors should rely on traditions that highlight originality and quality. Quality, used as a benchmark or established as a tradition, provides a most appealing and rewarding trademark all its own.

> *"They say the whole is greater than the sum of the parts it's made of."*
> —Stephen Schwartz

THE FINAL CURTAIN

The end of a school year is often awash in tradition. Many choirs present each senior to an audience or have a senior processional honoring individual singers. Our own school honors an outstanding student through the presentation of a "Spirit Stick." All students autograph an ordinary wooden dowel with colorful marking pens. This dowel is then presented to the student who has most clearly exhibited the ideals of devoted service to the group. An award can also be created to honor parent and grandparent dedication to choir activities.

As each new tradition becomes an old one, the choral program assumes an identity unique to its students and directors. Through the addition of each new idea, a group develops its own seal of originality. The blending of old and new traditions unique to each group develops a sense of belonging and pride, and this in turn engenders the commitment and loyalty of its members.

> *"All our dreams can come true, if we have the courage to pursue them."*
> —Walt Disney

Each choral director has distinct ideas, unique to his or her choral experiences, from which traditions will evolve. Traditions play an important part in the emotional ties students have to the choral program. Building these traditions, nurturing them and allowing them to evolve is one step toward the development of an excellent choral program.

SOME PRACTICAL SUGGESTIONS:
1. When new to a program, determine which traditions are important to students. It is essential to value and emphasize well established traditions. Even in a struggling program, there will be traditions that are important to students and parents. Be sensitive and wait awhile before bringing new traditions to the group. Be very hesitant to eliminate any valued traditions.
2. Research special traditions valued by colleagues and their choirs. Incorporate these ideas or modify them to suit your needs. In a neighboring school, there is a tradition where each student presents the director with a rose following the senior processional. This is an excellent idea that may be impractical in very large choirs, but could be adopted in smaller groups. For 20 years, another colleague has opened the holiday concert with a candlelit Christmas processional. The use of fire is prohibited in many schools but pen flashlights may work well instead. Ask colleagues about their special traditions, modify them to meet your needs or adopt them as your own.
3. Make the choir's traditions a topic for frequent discussion. Build pride by emphasizing the importance of your own traditions.
4. Involve students in the decision to alter a tradition. Consider their input seriously.

Nothing was more upsetting to Tevye than to find his traditions threatened by the outside world. Clinging to his traditional Jewish values and beliefs provided the anchor that he needed. His traditions gained additional importance because they were also important to his community, the people of Anatevka. Traditions are an integral part of any fellowship, including the community developed through choral singing. They are the glue of continuity that bonds a choral program together. Caring for and nurturing choral traditions makes it less difficult to navigate the road to excellence.

AUDITION SHEET

Name _____ Grade _____

Will you accept any role given to you? _____

Will we encounter any problems with absences? _____ Job? _____

Are you coachable? _____

Vocal Skill	5	4	3	2	1	*Range* _____
Physical Appropriateness	5	4	3	2	1	
Acting Potential	5	4	3	2	1	

Experience: 1. Prior Musicals _____

2. Choir Experience _____

3. Other _____

Callback   Yes   No

Leading Role   _____

_____

_____

Sample Audition Sheet

CHAPTER SIX

RECRUITING

Where the Boys Are

Wen attracting singers to a choir, the best recruiting tool is always the excellence of the program. Against tremendous odds, an outstanding program will prosper and thrive because players want to be on a winning team. No matter the circumstances under which a program begins, if a winning streak is sustained, and prospective members perceive repeated victories, the choir will grow.

How does a struggling or beginning program (the kind most in need of successful recruiting) use excellence as a recruiting tool? When faced with adversity (as are most in the arts today) the director committed to excellence plays the hand he or she is dealt. Given a choir of 10, the ambitious director produces quality music, creating a starting point from which to build a larger and more successful program. Working in a remote geographic region, the committed director uses the area's sparse resources to an advantage, fashioning a program that is the center of community life. The list of difficulties can be long, including many legitimate obstacles that block the path to success. As choir directors dedicated to educating our students and the community in the art of music, we must not consider these obstacles insurmountable.

> *"Success is failure turned inside out*
> *The silver tint of the clouds of doubt*
> *And you never can tell how close you are*
> *It may be near when it seems so far.*
> *So stick to the fight when you're hardest hit*
> *It's when things seem worse, That you must not quit."*
> —Unknown

RECOMMENDATIONS FOR RECRUITING:
Community Visibility

Since excellence is a choir director's best recruiting tool, demonstrating the program's excellence is a great way to increase participation. Performances in the community allow a choir to demonstrate musical success. A choir that performs regularly for community and club functions advertises its existence and quality. Once word spreads that a choir is available for activities such as holiday caroling, most communities will provide more than enough opportunities to spread the gospel of success.

One of the most powerful influences in a young person's life is a concerned parent. Aim to influence those parents. Mothers and fathers who witness a worthwhile choral program will encourage their children to become involved and, later, to stay involved. Performances aimed at area parents are worthwhile because the reward is excited singers sustained by parental support and chances are great that those same parents will become active and positive choir boosters once their children are involved.

Face to Face

In any student's decision making process, teacher contact is critical. Just when young people are apprehensive about their abilities, words of confidence and encouragement can offer a student direction and support. Many parents and students struggle with decisions about a course of study. Most families appreciate information on the opportunities available. Also valuable is an assessment of the student's potential for musical success. A brief letter sent to all incoming students is an effective way to reach prospective parents and students. A simple note can explain that choir is available to anyone interested, reassuring those who are apprehensive about a private audition. If it is possible to garner teacher recommendations, a separate letter can be sent to selected students informing them of a teacher recommendation. While it may take time and effort to contact all incoming students every year, the payback can be substantial.

> "Science and math may be the brain of our curriculum, and we cannot do without it. But arts is the heart. And we can't do without that, either."
> —Donna Shalala, Secretary of Health, Education and Welfare

Use contacts within the school setting to simplify the mechanics of such a mailing. Cultivate friendships in the guidance or business office where mailing labels are easily printed. Secretaries in the front office can facilitate a large mailing; the choir department can offer to sort and count envelopes so that a bulk mailing is possible. (This avoids what may be seen as prohibitive postage costs.) It pays to get the word out, and to make as many personal contacts as possible.

Friends Forever

At the high school level, friendship is often a significant factor in a student's decision to participate in choir. Young people are more likely to enroll in choral activities if they see older friends and classmates involved in the group. Encourage younger students to attend high school concerts, and when it is difficult to bring potential recruits to a concert, opt for taking the choir to them.

Elementary school tours are a practical avenue for reaching potential young singers, although in some situations travel time during the school day may be restricted. We found this time restriction enforced rigorously one year at our school, but refused to give up the contacts made through frequent grade school performances. With a few phone calls to the elementary schools and some flexibility regarding dates, it was possible to travel locally during the regular choir period. The choir could travel 15 minutes, sing a 30 minute concert and return within a total of 60 minutes. Because there was no disruption to the school curriculum or schedule, the administration was pleased, and contact was maintained with potential singers. Such a concession was somewhat disruptive to the choir's own schedule, but the compromise paid off in increased enrollments from the elementary graduates.

> "Make new friends but keep the old;
> Those are silver, these are gold.
> New-made friendships, like new wine,
> Age will mellow and refine."
> —Joseph Parry

CANDID CAMERA

Directors know from experience that music offers a strong emotional attraction to the young performer. Whether student, amateur or professional, the singer will find that music has a tremendous emotional appeal. When a director creates a fascination with music's emotional possibilities, often the potential singer is intrigued and will pursue the choral experience further.

> "Music is powerful, complex – a spirit beyond the reach of man's reasoning."
> —Eph Ehly

The following idea was presented at a Wisconsin state music convention. The details can be adapted to fit any particular situation, preserving the original intent: to use visual images that depict the personal interaction and friendships that are a part of any successful choral experience. Using candid shots of the choir, assemble a ten minute slide show. With New Age piano music, or a friendship song performed live for background music, compile a series of slides showing choir students in a myriad of activities. Viewers should see choir members singing, dancing, playing, sight-seeing, laughing, hugging, joking, and smiling. Conspicuous in the shots should be prominent members of the student population. Football players clad in jerseys, cheerleaders in uniform, or the show choir in group T-shirts are effective recruiting images when pictured throughout the presentation.

There are numerous opportunities for presenting such a slide show to potential choir members. As freshmen registration approaches, send choir seniors out to the eighth grade classes, armed with the slide show. Presented with little or no commentary, the slide show can be followed by a question and answer session. The appeal of this particular recruiting tool is that students speak to students.

The show can be incorporated into each year's final concert. While serving as a visual review of the year's activities, it also provides an added opportunity to interest new students in the program.

Many schools host an open house just prior to class registration. Use this opportunity to run the slide show at a booth where other choir information is also available.

Make the community aware that quality music fosters friendships and fun. So much of music's value lies in the extra-musical benefits gained through the experience. Use this appeal to good advantage.

WHERE ARE THOSE BOYS?

What about them? Sometimes a pre-existing stigma about boys in the arts presents an obstacle to recruiting. A female choral director may feel especially hampered in recruiting young men and overcoming the cultural perception that singing is not a masculine pursuit.

In handling this touchy subject, a practical (and usually effective) approach is one that appeals to the boys' idea of masculinity. Affiliate with and liken the choir to athletics, not only because the analogy will appeal to boys but because the comparison is a valid one. Remind all singers to "Sing like athletes," and that, "Singers must be in good shape to sing

> *"Most people give up just when they're about to achieve success. They quit on the one yard line. They give up at the last minute of the game one foot from a winning touchdown."*
>
> —H. Ross Perot

well." Emphasize the physical stamina needed to sing well. Expand the comparison between music and athletics to include a discussion of team dynamics, and the necessity for team work and cooperation in both fields.

Choir members who achieve outside the music setting can and should be recognized. Assign leadership positions to singers who are also leaders in athletics (male or female). Post newspaper articles recognizing athletic team success when choir members are featured. Professional sports offer another avenue for comparison. Draw parallels between choir activities and those of major sports endeavors.

> *"Nothing in the world can take the place of persistence. Talent will not; nothing is more common than unsuccessful men with talent. Genius will not; education will not. Persistence and determination alone are omnipotent."*
> —Calvin Coolidge

Making choir similar to an athletic endeavor helps to put male members at ease. These men will then spread the word about the success of choir. But don't rely solely on those already involved. Potential male singers can be found everywhere: in study halls, cafeteria lines or band practices. Students with the ability to sing are ubiquitous and personal contact with them is invaluable. Some light-hearted banter such as, "You know, only the handsomest men can sing in choir and you definitely qualify!" can open the door to conversation and more serious recruiting.

PROCEED WITH CAUTION

One word of caution — Young ladies may seem already sold on the value of choir. Never undervalue that participation. Resist the tendency to pay more attention, or pander to the young men. Treating all fairly and valuing both sexes is essential. Also, never underestimate the ability of girls to attract boys to choir. If only a few boys are enrolled in choir, send young women on a mission. They will almost certainly be able to bring young men to the choral program with a little coercion and much flattery. If all else fails, stress that with almost no homework and no tests, this class can aid the grade point average!

Sometimes it is not easy to measure the results of recruiting efforts. One never knows which recruiting device may have piqued the interest of a potential singer. The only option is to use as many opportunities as possible to gain visibility, create positive public relations, and reach students on a personal level.

SOME PRACTICAL SUGGESTIONS:

1. Perform frequently in the community. Offer to perform at Rotary meetings or other club gatherings.
2. Appear often at local elementary and middle schools. Ask if they are hosting a Fine Arts Day where the choir could be featured.
3. Invite middle school students to the high school auditorium for a dress rehearsal of the musical or a concert.
4. Ask elementary or middle school music teachers for student recommendations. Follow up with a letter to the students and their parents, issuing an invitation to join in the special experiences offered by choral activities.
5. Send an open letter to all incoming students a few weeks before class registration. Make it known that choir is open to anyone interested. Make all feel welcome.
6. Create a slide show that features the unique appeal of your program. Feature students having fun, emphasizing that choir is a comfortable, pleasant, successful place to be.
7. You are also a coach! Don't waste time competing against athletics. Assume that singers can do both. Affiliate with athletics and show an interest in sports. For many students, athletics is as important as music and both activities teach many of the same values.
8. Offer extra credit to present members who recruit new singers.
9. Visitor day is a valid recruiting tool. Invite study hall students to visit. Encourage choir members to personally host a visitor for a day.
10. Make the choral product a quality one. This is the most powerful recruiting tool of all.

> *"Why teach? To share what we know, to improve the quality of human existence."*
> —Eph Ehly

COME ONE, COME ALL!

Recruiting is vital to most choral programs because without active efforts, numbers can dwindle to dangerous lows. It may seem that recruiting efforts steal valuable rehearsal hours, but unless one takes the need to recruit seriously, there will be no choir to rehearse. A small choir of excellent quality will impress potential recruits, but a large choir of excellent quality will be even more impressive. Numbers count. Do whatever it takes to sell the choral program to young people. Make a plan and follow through. See that choir is a credited class and not an extra-curricular activity. Enlist the help you need from parents, the elementary music teachers, guidance staff – anyone who can help bring young people to the arts.

Dear Parent of an Eighth Grader:

Congratulations on your eighth grader's anticipated graduation this spring! We wish you and your son or daughter success at the High School.

On the recommendation of your child's elementary music teacher, we invite your son or daughter to be a member of the High School Choral program. While choir at the freshman level is open to anyone interested in singing, your child's name has been recommended as one who would be successful in choir.

We presently have 65 freshman boys and 80 freshman girls in our program. We hope to see your student as a member of next year's freshman choir.

We look forward to an exciting year with our freshman class. Please call if you have any questions or we can help you in any way.

Sincerely,

Your Directors

"Why arts in education? Why education at all? The purpose of education is not simply to inform but to enrich and enlighten, to provide insights into life as it has been led and as it may be led. No element of the curriculum is better suited to that task than arts education. Whether we think about music, the performing arts, the plastic arts, whether we think about appreciation or performance, the arts take us beyond pragmatic concerns of the moment and give us a glimpse of human possibility."

— David T. Kearns
Chairman and Chief Executive Officer of Xerox Corporation

Sample Recruiting Letter

Dear Parents:

Having recently completed a very successful and rewarding semester of choral activities, we are looking ahead to next year. It is with pleasure that we invite your student to be part of Mixed Choir. This choir is open to any sophomore, but we particularly recommend your student to sing with this fine choir. We are looking forward to working again with your son or daughter next year.

Sincerely,

Your Directors

Sample Recruiting Letter

The Choral Department invites you to consider membership in the Show Choir.

Please consider the following information when making your decision to become a member:

1. It is both a great honor and a great responsibility to perform with our Show Choir. Our reputation of continued excellence is the direct result of hard work and dedication from its members.

2. Show Choir camp is held during one full week in August. Since we learn our songs and our dance routines in camp, everyone MUST be in attendance.

3. The school does not fund our trips or our costumes. We provide fundraising to defray these costs but parents and students need to be aware of them before committing to membership.

4. Show Choir requires much out-of-school time. Members rehearse after school, after sports and sometimes on weekends. Please realize that Show Choir is a wonderful experience that represents a large commitment of time and energy.

Please sign the form below if you wish to continue the audition process. We are honored to have you share your talent with our choral department.

• •

My parents and I understand the responsibilities and obligations of belonging to the Show Choir and would consider it a great honor to be part of the ensemble.

Student _____

Parent _____

Sample Release Form

CHAPTER SEVEN

BRAGGING AS AN ART FORM

Sales Experience Mandatory

One February morning, our favorite band director was visiting the choir office. There was much excitement about the choir's progress that year, and we were sharing our pride with him. Because we brag regularly about our choir students, the band director was somewhat skeptical. Clearly he needed verification as to the group's excellence. "Has anyone else heard them?" he asked. "Of course!" we responded. "We invited our secretary to hear them two days ago, the custodian came by yesterday and a math teacher visited today. They all agreed that our singers are going to be great!"

> "Always be generous with praise and cautious with criticism."
> —Unknown

The art of bragging about student accomplishment is one well worth cultivating because its rewards are far reaching. Bragging is a way to disseminate information about the choir, increase recruiting efforts, and build confidence among choir members. One successful device within the art of bragging is to invite colleagues, custodians, support staff and administration to the classroom on a regular basis. After the choir has sung, guests may be invited to comment. Outsiders are usually not extremely critical and their praise of the choir's progress can be reinforced by the director's positive observations. The praise must be genuine and accurate, allowing the director to also note areas needing improvement.

Encourage colleagues to share the choir's success. A fellow teacher is usually flattered when asked to critique the choir, and often enjoys being included in the activities. Good will is often engendered through this sharing of ideas. Those who are familiar with the choir's good work may also become ambassadors for the choir throughout the community. We need not be in search of excellence alone, and an in-house cheering squad can do wonders for encouragement and morale, our own as well as our students'.

Most directors are uncomfortable bragging about themselves, but bragging about students puts the focus elsewhere. The local newspaper is an appropriate avenue where the community can learn about the choir's successes. Write press releases for the local media and mention often the names of students, parents and other partners. Preparing press releases is a time consuming but essential task if one wants to ensure that music receives its share of coverage. Creating respect and admiration for choral groups is usually the director's responsibility and it's an important one since the community will only know what is published and made public. The venues for bragging are everywhere. Student accomplishments can be heralded in morning announcements, the school newspaper, and the local press. Special events require special attention and the director needs to advertise these happenings by using every publicity angle possible.

> *"It is better to deserve honors and not have them, than to have them and not deserve them."*
> —Mark Twain

When our choir needed a regular, dependable method of reaching and informing parents, a newsletter was born. No one at the New York Times feels at all threatened by this one-page experiment with journalism but the newsletter is informative, creative and timely. It is called the "Choral Chronicle" and is sent four times a year to each student's home. It is easy to blatantly boast about students when parents are the only audience and in addition to some bragging, the newsletter is an important vehicle for information about concerts, auditions, and other events.

> *"The people who get on in this world are the people who get up and look for the circumstances they want, and, if they can't find them, make them.*
> —George Bernard Shaw

To increase the perception that choral music is successful and important, credit student achievement often. Directors are salespeople. Their product is a quality choir that sings aesthetic, exciting, passion-filled music. As salespeople, we can sell younger singers on the idea of excellence by noting the achievement of more mature singers. We can offer this year's musical cast the example of excellence demonstrated by last year's cast. As successes increase, it is vital that they are discussed, highlighted, and used as a springboard for further accomplishments. Continually crediting the work of each group creates a pride in accomplishment and a dedication to continued achievement. Bragging is merely the refined art of accentuating the positive.

Setting the tone for praise of student accomplishment can begin at the top. On the opening day of school music directors can introduce each other to students not as teachers, but as "artists-in-residence." Call students' attention to each director's special skills as musicians, actors, and professionals. The respect and praise we afford each other as directors sets the tone for our students.

Our society places great value on the efforts of athletes and sometimes the arts seem ignored or overlooked. We can certainly be forgiven for feelings of frustration and bitterness, but resentment doesn't even the score. Instead, the director must don the hat of publicity manager and call attention to important musical efforts. The work of students should not be a well-kept secret. A successful choral program has a director who habitually publicizes musical achievements. The rewards more than justify the efforts.

SOME PRACTICAL SUGGESTIONS:

1. Appoint one student from each choir to serve as publicity chairperson for that group. Make it his or her responsibility to put news of choir activities on school bulletins and announcements.
2. Have a press release form printed and use it to notify local newspapers. Find someone at the newspaper office who will insure that press releases are published.
3. Obtain phone numbers for television contact people. Call when special events warrant extra publicity and extra bragging.
4. Videotape concerts and run them on local cable stations. Many parents videotape performances and are usually happy to share them.
5. Publish a choral newsletter. Journalism students can help with the layout and printing. Students can be in charge of the mailing.
6. Never miss a chance to inform the public about student success. Note every milestone and improvement with praise.
7. Take pictures of the choir and use them to advertise the choir's activities. Create bulletin boards in the choir room and around the school building. Decorate a display case with choir awards and pictures. Send photos to the local paper to accompany important press releases.

The refined art of bragging yields an array of excellent results. The benefits include improved recruiting results, positive public relations for the department, and increased self-esteem for the choral groups. When accurate information reaches the community about a wide array of choral activities, and when choral events are prominently credited by the school and the community, accomplishing even higher goals becomes considerably easier.

The Choral Chronicle

September 1994 Arrowhead High School Choral Music Department

Chorale Chosen to Represent State in D.C.

*T*he 1994/95 Broadway Bound Chorale has been chosen by Music Celebrations International to represent the state of Wisconsin in Washington D.C. in a festival celebrating the 50th anniversary of the end of World War II. Bands and choirs from every state in the union and provinces of all allied nations will convene next spring in Washington, London and Paris. Performances over a three month period will honor veterans, both living and dead, and will commemorate the heroism of that war.

Victory Celebration!!

The Chorale will be in Washington April 14 - 21, 1995 touring, performing and attending the celebrations. They will re-visit the homeless shelter called Martha's Table and present the shelter with gifts. Many families will accompany the group on their spring tour.

Concert Choir to Perform at Carroll College Festival

*T*he members of the North Concert Choir will be off to a very exciting start and a very early one too! Directors Catherine Pfeiler and Nancy Jorgensen have announced that the choir is to be one of the guest choirs performing at the Carroll College Festival on Saturday, October 8, 1994. The concert time is 7:00 P.M. in Shattuck Auditorium in Waukesha. Members of the Sophomore South Select will also attend, serving as ushers and assisting North Choir. The evening promises to be an exciting one. Also performing will be the Carroll College choir and a Festival Choir directed by William Hatcher of the University of Iowa, featuring select singers from around the state, including 16 of Arrowhead's best singers.

With Hope to Share

*T*he vision - a world without hunger and hopelessness; the visionary - nationally known choreographer and choral clinician, John Jacobson. The project is called "America Sings!" and ten AHS singers and director Catherine Pfeiler traveled to Washington, D.C. the week of July 1 - 6 to learn about "America Sings" through Jacobson's *America Singposium*. The group crammed an incredible amount of diverse experiences into the week, singing, dancing and performing, working in homeless shelters, preparing meals for street people, and meeting people from across the nation, Canada and Japan. In addition to seeing the musical, *The Hot Mikado*, the group toured the capital, watched the U.S. Senate debate, and saw the monuments to freedom that are Washington, D.C.

The purpose of the trip was to learn how the arts can be used to help those who have lost hope. Bringing back ideas on how to change our small part of the world for the better, the group will use as its theme for the year the motto of "America Sings!" - " To those who have lost hope, from kids with hope to share." David Brown, Ryan Rosenberg, Michael Palovcsik, David Ries, Nate Pautz, Catherine Chapman, Mary Liz Kleis, Shelly Christopherson and Christine Emmerich were chosen to represent the AHS choral program and made the unforgettable trip. The group has pledged not to forget the faces of need and hunger they saw while only six blocks from our nation's capital. Each month they and the members of the AHS choirs, including the show choir, will organize projects to help others. The first project was a community drive to collect school supplies for children whose families aren't financially able to provide. Other projects will include stocking area food pantries and donating gifts for needy children at Holiday time.

A Vision of A Better World

Sample Choral Newsletter – Page 1

News Plus

Can't Escape the Rhythm
Show Choir Camp

Summer did not find AHS Show Choir team members idle. The summer found the members of the AHS Show Choir studying two very different types of dance. Many took tap lessons in June and July and learned the country line dances so popular to the world of country music. The culmination of the many hours of work came when Show Choir Camp convened the week of August 9 - 13.

Sixty singer/dancers, band members and crew spent an intense week learning their 1994-95 competitive show. They performed for family, friends and alumni at the Camp Show, Saturday, August 13. The show included the opener, "Taking Heaven By Storm," choreographed by Indianapolis choreographer Damon Brown. The ballad, from the musical *1776* is "Mama, Look Sharp". The tap extravaganza is from the movie *Tap* and is choreographed by Milwaukee dance instructor Jenny Toth. The finale is a country music medley choreographed by Broadway Bound alumni Alison Spakowitz and Patrick Minkley.

Highlighting the camp, hosted by Coach Pfeiler, was the arrival of the beautiful new costumes, props, T-shirts and garment bags. Special thanks to all parents who provided refreshments all week and especially to Mrs. Berner, Mrs. David and Mrs. Audley. Thanks also to all students and parents who hosted evening practices!

Parents' Night!

All parents of the 1994-95 AHS Show Choir are invited to a special concert in their honor. Tuesday, October 11, the student members will introduce their parents, grandparents and family members at Parents' Night. They will also perform for the parents, wearing their new costumes. A short meeting will follow and refreshments will be served. The concert, which will take place in the theater, begins at 7:00 P.M. .

Debut Performance

All Arrowhead choirs will make their first 1994/95 appearance on October 17. The concert, which will be in the North Campus gym, will feature the Treble Choir, South Mixed Choir, South Select Ensemble, North Concert Choir and the Broadway Bound Show Choir. As in the past, choir members should dress appropriately for this formal event. Men are to wear dress slacks, dress shirt, conventional tie, sport coat, socks, dress shoes, and a belt. Ladies are to wear a dress or skirt and top. Skirt length is to be mid-calf. Plan to arrive early to secure a parking place and a good seat.

Performance Dates

Show Choir Competitions:
February 11 - La Crosse Logan
February 28 - Mooreville, Indiana
March 11 - Mt Zion, Illinois
March 25 - AHS Invitational

Broadway Bound Chorale Trips:
April 12 - Dorian Invitational, Decorah Iowa
May 12 - 13 America Sings! Chicago, Illinois

Show Choir Trip to Washington D.C
April 14 - 21.

Other Broadway Bound commitments(not including caroling)
January 18 - School Board Convention
January 21 - Madison - Veterans Group
April 27 - Wisconsin Singers Show

Choir Concerts:
October 17 - Fall Concert
December 22 - Winter Concert
May 9 - South Final Concert
May 15 - North Final Concert

North Concert Choir Trips:
October 8 - Carroll College
TBA - Kansas City, Missouri

Other Obligations:
February 4 - Honors Auditions

March 4 - Distirct Solo and Ensemble

April 29 - State Solo and Ensemble

May 28 - Commencement

Sample Choral Newsletter – Page 2

PRESS RELEASE

For Immediate Release   For More Information Contact:

_____

_____
# # #

Sample Press Release

CHAPTER EIGHT

NO CHOIR IS AN ISLAND
Politics and Priorities

Music has long been recognized and revered as one of the most powerful forms of communication. When words fail, mankind turns to music to express the deepest thoughts and the most intense emotions. Most directors hope that long past the time when students have forgotten the alto part to "Cantate Domino," they will remember the immeasurable power of music to convey hope and despair, longing and contentment, joy and sadness. Those who participate in choir discover the importance of music's unique ability to touch emotions and feelings.

> *"I would rather have three minutes of wonderful than a lifetime of nothing special."*
> —"Terms of Endearment"

TIMES OF JOY AND TIMES OF SORROW

Just as music reflects life's deepest and most complicated emotions, so does it mirror life's day-to-day existence. Visual art reflects life, and music does that also in its songs of love and sacred hymns, work chanteys and bawdy drinking songs, humorous ditties and jubilant celebrations of life. Every significant event in our world today includes music. Be it a local sporting event or the Olympics, wedding or funeral, commencement ceremony or the inauguration of a president, music plays a part. Because music so completely pervades our culture, when we immerse our students completely in the experience of music, we introduce them to life's experiences as well.

> *"Opportunity...Often it comes disguised in the form of misfortune, or temporary defeat."*
> —Napoleon Hill

Given music's power to communicate ideas and emotions, and its omnipresence in the world today, the choir setting is the perfect forum for discussions about our world. To the many teenagers for whom the high school curriculum seems irrelevant, the choir classroom is the perfect place to initiate discussions on important topics. Sometimes the right moment just appears, and cannot be planned. We turned the television on during choir one day to watch the launching of the spaceship Challenger. Instead of celebrating the first American teacher in space, we witnessed the horror of death as the entire crew was annihilated in mid-air. Only one thing seemed the appropriate interruption of that moment of tragedy. The 130 voice choir of juniors and seniors sang "Precious Lord, Take My Hand" and then left the room in silence. Words could not explain the unspeakable. Only music could offer some small comfort, and a meaningful response to the tragedy.

There are other times when world events demand attention, and a planned discussion can answer questions and lessen students' anxieties. In the middle of the Desert Storm crisis, many students were confused. Since most were not in classes where this frightening situation was discussed, we briefly explained the recent history of Middle East conflicts and the involvement of the United States, and attempted to ease their anxieties over this national ordeal. While most elementary students had a classroom teacher available for such discussions, many high school students found choir to be the only class where this topic was discussed.

> "It is the obligation we have been given. It is to not turn out the same. It is to grow, to accomplish -- to change the world!
> —Stephen Sondheim, Merrily We Roll Along

IN TRAINING FOR LIFE

In almost every American school, students are offered instruction about drug and alcohol abuse. A director's relationship with choir students is often unique and can be used to further this awareness. While stressing the educational rather than the punitive, the choir director adds another adult voice to a mighty chorus of caution. Conscientious directors must help change our society's attitudes about excessive drinking and other drugs and alert students to the damaging dangers of it.

Since many activities associated with choir are extra-curricular, choir members are often subject to a code of conduct similar to athletic codes. The threat of suspension from a performance can be a powerful tool in preventing at least some of the casual high school drinking that occurs. When a group performance is canceled because of an individual's code violations, peer pressure to conform to accepted standards becomes even more powerful.

Music booster organizations can be effective in influencing students to adopt a healthy lifestyle free of drugs, alcohol, and inappropriately intimate behavior. At a parent booster meeting one year, the topic of teen hotel parties was discussed. It became apparent that students were hosting unsupervised parties, while parents assumed these parties were chaperoned. Because the booster parents felt comfortable with one another, they agreed to contact each other in the future before allowing their children to attend such gatherings. The students could no longer convince their parents that unchaperoned parties were supervised, and parents were no longer hesitant to check with each other on party details.

Despite our best efforts, life's tragedies are sometimes unavoidable. Recently, a student at our school took his own life. The tragic suicide affected every one of our students, even those who were only briefly acquainted with the young man. Surely learning the bass part of "We Be Three Poor Mariners" and the listening lesson on shanty songs from *Chanticleer's* latest recording were set aside. A frank discussion of depression ensued. We attempted to convince the students of life's irreplaceable worth. Assuming the role of guidance counselor, we urged our singers to confide in us or other adults if they ever contemplated suicide or knew of someone who did. On such a tragic day, it was imperative that the planned curriculum be suspended to teach an even more important lesson.

Choir directors possess the unique opportunity to maintain a special closeness with students. If students' trust can be won, young people may look to a respected director for needed guidance. Though music education alone is an enormous task, and it may seem overwhelming just to cover the academic basics of music history, theory, sight reading and performance skills, students deserve more. They deserve an education in what music is really all about. The search for excellence must not become so narrow that we fail to allow time for a discussion of world events or topics relevant to the lives of young people.

> *"Now is the time to seize the day!"*
> —Jack Feldman, *Newsies*

SOME PRACTICAL SUGGESTIONS:

1. Find time each Friday to discuss the choir code of conduct. Anticipating free time available on the weekend, discuss the need for mature decisions regarding time spent with friends.
2. Watch for television programs that deal with topics of interest to teens. Alert students to news programs about teen drinking, drug abuse, or teen pregnancy.
3. Clip short newspaper articles to share with a class.
4. Initiate class discussions about timely topics. To make conversation easier, begin a sentence and have volunteers finish it (e.g., I can help my friends resist the pressure to drink by . . .).
5. When a major world news event breaks, mention it in class, offer an explanation if needed, and allow time for questions and discussion. Encourage students to be informed about the world around them.
6. Because choir often includes a wide range of the student population, make it a place to discuss issues of racial and ethnic tolerance.

> *"Destiny is not a matter of chance; it is a matter of choice. It is not something to be waited for; but, rather something to be achieved."*
> —William Jennings Bryan

7. Take note when an important event features music and mention it to the choir. So much of daily life includes music, but students may need their attention drawn to specific examples.
8. Celebrate the choir's music. Prepare students for emotions they may experience at a concert. Emphasize their obligation to the audience and to the emotions the music was intended to convey. Stress the singular power of a choir to communicate feelings and emotions through song.

The unique communicative nature of music allows us to contribute to our students' lives as no one else can. Directors have the opportunity to enrich their singers' lives not only because of the special power of music to examine and engender emotions, but because of the special personal relationship a choir director can have with students.

Directors are also people and citizens of the world who struggle with life and learn side by side with their singers. Music is not a discipline isolated from everyday life. Directors who capitalize on this fact enrich their students' lives forever.

OUR CODE OF CONDUCT

OUR CODE PROHIBITS:

1. Possession or use of any controlled substance, alcohol, or tobacco; assault, theft or possession of stolen property.

2. Being at parties or gatherings where alcohol or illegal substances are being used.

3. Being in cars where drinking, smoking, or unbecoming conduct is taking place.

SMART IDEAS:

1. Call our hot line if you find yourself anywhere trouble could occur.
   We will see that you have a safe ride home.

2. Don't attend gatherings where parents are not present.

3. Learn to say "no." Remember how special you are to all of us. Think before you act. Don't let our team down!

Sample Code of Conduct

CHAPTER NINE

CONTESTS AND COMPETITIONS
All That Glitters Isn't Gold

T here is no better teacher than a really big mistake, but no one can learn everything by trial and error. We all must use the experience of others to help us avoid costly errors.

WINNING ISN'T EVERYTHING

The following is a true anecdote regarding competition, retold in the interest of helping others learn by another's mistake. Our choir had a reputation for

> *"The true meaning of winning is discovering the best in all of us."*
> —Olympic Creed

seeking out and enjoying competition. When the phone call came from California that our choir had been chosen to represent Wisconsin in national competition, everyone was ecstatic. The second reaction was cold fear, of course, but that came much later. The next eight months were devoted to doing everything possible to win this national competition. In Wisconsin, where devotion to the winning ethic of Vince Lombardi dominates all competitive ventures, few argued with the established goal. The choir rehearsed an inordinate amount of time, practicing over both Holiday and Spring break, and in the face of such a vigorous schedule, two students dropped the competitive venture at semester. Every learning opportunity focused on a strategy that would win in Los Angeles. When the dust settled in May and we were forced to buy an extra airline seat to accommodate the nine trophies for the trip home, many felt an admirable goal had been attained. First runner-up in a national competition by anyone's standards is grand. The goal was achieved; however, the wrong goal had been established. In retrospect the pride in winning remains, but it is regrettable that so much time was invested into an eight minute performance. The students were pushed too long and hard for the wrong reasons. This emphasis on winning at all costs was a huge mistake.

There is tremendous value in competitions. While some argue that music should never be competitive, there are advantages to the occasional competitive endeavor. Obviously many aspects of music are competitive whether one likes it or not, and students must be prepared to compete, not only in the world of music, but in the real world. A

> *"Winning is not a some-time thing. It is an all-time thing. You don't do things right once in a while; you do them right all the time."*
> —Vince Lombardi

reasoned approach to the competitive arena acknowledges the positive role that competition can play in a program, and is wary about the negative role that it can play.

Choirs should compete to learn. Hearing the opinions of judges and clinicians and listening to the advice they offer is essential to professional growth. Students are motivated by the sure knowledge that their group will be heard, and seen; and a director soon realizes that students work harder with this in mind. The chance to stand in the winner's circle, the chance to bring home trophies and awards all play a part in this motivation to be sure. They are the useful by-products of competition, but the real and lasting value of competitive events includes seeing a new way of doing something, hearing a wonderful new song, and working together toward a common goal. It is always the director's responsibility to ensure that the positive aspects of competition are accentuated, and the negative aspects avoided or downplayed. It is essential to guarantee students a measure of positive growth and well-being within the competitive setting.

SOME PRACTICAL SUGGESTIONS:
1. Avoid making one single competition, no matter how prestigious, an entire year's focus. Make it one of many quality music experiences offered by the choral program.
2. Emphasize that the trophies and travel surrounding a competitive venture are secondary to everything learned along the way. Stress the importance of musical learning and team effort, rather than the possibility of gold.
3. Keep a realistic perspective. When judgment is passed upon a group, it is a judgment of the director's teaching as well. Think of it as another chance to learn, rather than report card day!

4. Avoid placing too much stock in one person's opinion. Clinicians and judges are only human. They are well-intentioned, usually knowledgeable and hopefully objective, but by the very nature of the art, there is room for differences of opinion.

5. Insist on good deportment and impeccable sportsmanship at competitive events. Establish high expectations for the group as spectators as well as competitors. Knowing how to be a gracious winner or loser requires skill. Spending an inordinate time in the winners' circle or celebrating with a vengeance is as inappropriate in the music arena as it is in the sports arena.

6. Spend time after the competitive event discussing everything learned, everything that improved along the way, and everything for which you feel pride. Without this important follow-up, the emphasis might wrongly be placed on the win or loss. The emphasis is never to dominate others, but to learn and to share.

> *"All great achievements require time."*
> —David Joseph Schwartz

7. Students take their cue from the director so it is important to be honorable and admirable in accepting criticism. Avoid blame-laying or excuse-making. Always show attitudes worthy of imitation.

8. Be a class act. Wherever you go, wherever you place in the competition, make a good impression. Make friends, encourage students to do the same, and remind parents that they must be good examples too!

Anyone choosing to participate in the competitive arena is taking a risk. Many, fearing critical assessment, never compete, thus denying their choirs an opportunity that is a powerful teaching tool when used in the proper perspective and with the proper emphasis. A director must insist that a competition enhance educational objectives, and is not tarnished by excessive partisanship. Those who compete for the sake of learning will not fret over a disappointing score. Veteran competitors relate many wonderful experiences that happened at events where the group didn't win.

> *"We can't all do great things. We can only do small things with great love."*
> —Jim Kimmel

CLINICS, CAMPS AND CONVENTIONS

The non-competitive festival is tremendously valuable to a choral program. This unique opportunity hosted by colleges and universities offers small groups of students the chance to spend a day submerged in music with other students from the area. Often directed by nationally known conductors, students and teachers participate in a truly memorable musical experience. The small group that participates returns with excitement for quality literature, a reaffirmation of the importance of discipline and new musical knowledge ready to be shared. Don't miss these special days.

Encourage students to participate in summer camps and clinics. Not only will they have a wonderful learning experience but they will make new friends and gain added confidence in themselves and in their performance skills. Singers grow when exposed to a new approach and fresh ideas. No one director knows everything, but each director should know enough to encourage singers in a wide search for knowledge. As an added bonus, most singers hear their own director's ideas reiterated in a new way, giving added weight and importance to information they've already learned.

As educators embarking on a long professional life, it is important to constantly stay current and continue to learn. Directors must take their own advice to heart, and attend clinics, conventions and seminars that are crucial to continued learning. Even if some of the time spent in classes and workshops is not always pertinent, conversation and contact with other music educators is worthwhile. Important ideas are often discussed informally over dinner at a convention or a choral clinic. Old friendships can be renewed and new ones fostered through mutual participation in workshops, reading sessions, and conventions.

CONCERTS

Someone once said, "There are times that reward you for all the toil and tears." Sometimes those rewarding moments happen during competitive events or festival formats. Most often, however, these

> *"He has achieved success who has lived well, laughed often, and loved much."*
> —Unknown

moments happen at concerts. There is a certain magic about the home crowd, the home stage. Concerts are culminating activities and the public demonstration of all that has occurred in private rehearsal. As a choral director, one's job is to make concerts the most memorable musical happenings possible. Concerts are one's opportunity to put a unique mark on a choral program. Make it the mark of excellence.

SOME PRACTICAL SUGGESTIONS:
1. Keep concerts short and sweet. Patrons will leave wanting more and return eagerly for the next performance.
2. Cut selections that are not performance ready. Nothing can diminish confidence in a choral program quicker than a disastrous performance. If a piece is not adequately prepared, save it for another time.
3. A concert is a theatrical event. Carefully prepare the evening's script, set the stage, and see that technical props such as microphones and lighting are in working order. Be sure that all performers are aware of the evening's required concert attire.
4. Avoid speaking at concerts. If spoken introductions are used, students should deliver them. Make the singers the stars of the show.
5. If audience deportment is a problem, use program notes to thank the audience for not walking in and out during performances, for leaving crying babies at home and for their energetic and kind applause. The soft sell can work small miracles. If you are still not satisfied with audience behavior, do something about it. Teach each choir member about correct and acceptable behavior at concerts, hoping the message will reach the audience indirectly.
6. Honor parents at concerts whenever possible. Call attention to their continued support. Have the superintendent or principal on hand. By asking them to introduce you or to welcome the audience you imply their support for the choral program. Because they are already in attendance, they actually hear the choir and are often surprised and impressed by the performance.
7. Present concerts in conjunction with arts displays or theater arts. Building bridges with other departments and showing the interrelatedness of the arts is always time well spent.
8. Build concerts around themes. Grouping songs (Madrigal Madness, Folksong Fantasy, etc.) gives structure to a concert.
9. Cover a variety of time periods using strong teaching pieces but make the concert interesting and entertaining as well.

10. Put younger groups on the same concert with more experienced groups. Sing at least one song together. The younger singers will be inspired and motivated by the more experienced ensembles, parents will see the growth from year to year, and with more singers, the audience of parents and friends will be larger.

11. Invite elementary music teachers to secondary music concerts. Once aware of your program, they are more likely to encourage their charges to participate.

12. Hold receptions after important concerts. Take time to speak to parents.

13. Decorate for programs. Let everyone know that something very special is happening. Have quality printed programs on hand, take photographs and make video recordings. Do the necessary public relations to insure that a large, appreciative audience is on hand.

"There are moments that reward you for all the toil and tears."

14. Bring in guest artists to perform with students. Nothing inspires more than a professional singing with the choir. Singers will do an even better job with extra inspiration. Bring in guest conductors for the same good reasons.

Concerts, competitions, clinics. In teaching history or science one might successfully complete a career in education and never have need for them. Our unique field of music requires that we participate in these extra-curricular experiences. We will have moments that will reward a thousand times over as a result of these extra experiences.

The Road
(In Praise of Choir Clinics)

by Max V. Exner

They asked me to direct
the choir,
And wondered if I'd build a fire
To spark a crew of singers that
Was flagging, sagging,
singing flat.

I said I'd give the thing a try
Until they found another guy;
But that was many years ago
When I knew not what now
I know.

A simpler choice I could
have made,
Like moving mountains
with a spade,
Or catching flies with fire tongs
And leading frogs in sing-alongs.

The problems were, in
every case,
A mirror held before my face.
If notes on Sunday were
not right,
I'd missed the trouble
Wednesday night.
If rhythm fell into retreat,
It helped to sharpen up my beat;
The song was heavy on its feet.
To keep rehearsals up to pace,
Against myself I had to race;
The reason for a listless mood
Was often in my attitude;
The problem of small repertoire
Was loafing by the directoire!

I found a choir, to my chagrin,
A problem in self-discipline.
"A curve-ball," I declared, "a foul!"
And wanted to throw in the towel.

But then, one day, it came to me
That I was in good company:
That other folk had had to deal
With these same pups that
dogged my heel
I talked with them, they talked
with me,
And very soon I came to see
That my frustrations weren't
unique,
Which made the vista much
less bleak.

I asked what answers they
had found;
We traded questions all around,
To sniff out problems where
they lurk
And find what works and
doesn't work.

Oh, some were brilliant as the sky,
And some were just as dumb as I,
But every one of them in turn
Had learned a thing that I
could learn!

And since that time, with
those instructors,
I've left the ranks of "choir
conductors,"
To move each day, now slow,
now faster,
Toward the state of "choirmaster."

Dear Parent:

As the choir directors at the High School, we encourage our most talented students to audition for special opportunities that are available throughout the year. Because your son or daughter has shown exceptional talent as a singer and sight reader, we are sending the enclosed application for the Honors Project.

There are two choral groups available through audition to students in the state. The Honors Choir is a select group of 100 singers (25 sopranos, 25 altos, 25 tenors, 25 basses) that performs music from the standard repertoire of choral literature. The Honors Vocal Jazz Choir is a select group of 24 singers (6 sopranos, 6 altos, 6 tenors, 6 basses) that performs vocal jazz both a cappella and accompanied. Those chosen meet at Carroll College for four days in June to work with a nationally acclaimed conductor. Their work culminates in a performance at the State Music Convention in October.

The deadline for applications to audition for either of these groups is _____. Only the application and a $6.00 application fee are due at that time. The auditions take place at _____ in _____ on _____.

At the audition the student is required to perform a Class A solo, sing a sight reading example, and do a few range exercises. We are confident your son or daughter is ready for this audition, and are willing to help in any way possible.

If you have any questions, please call either one of us. Should you and your son or daughter decide to pursue this special opportunity, return the application and fee to school. We will sign and forward it to the state office. Thank you.

Sincerely,

Your Directors

Sample Choir Letter

CHAPTER TEN

ALL FOR ONE!
ONE FOR ALL!
Parents and Other Partners

Managing a choir department requires time, skill, and energy in a variety of areas. The talents necessary are wide ranging and diverse, requiring each director to be a business manager, an organization leader, a public relations chairperson, the motivational speaker, and a musical scholar. In considering the enormity of the position, one soon realizes it is not possible to personally administer every aspect of a successful program. The efficient choir director delegates duties and responsibilities; the wise director delegates while still retaining control where musical and many other critical decisions are concerned.

> *The Anatomy of an Organization:*
> 1. *Wish Bones*
> 2. *Jaw Bones*
> 3. *Knuckle Bones*
> 4. *Tail Bones*
> 5. *Back Bones*

In a successful program, the choir director sometimes functions less as a classroom teacher and more as business manager. With budgets tight, many choral programs are forced to fund raise and some are compelled to be self-supporting. Parents can help! To function in the competitive arena, many show choirs are forced to fund raise substantial amounts of money. It is understood that student members pick up some of the cost for personal expenses out of town (including food and hotel costs). Since the total price tag would be prohibitive if students were responsible for covering everything associated with membership in the group, a parent booster group often raises money to cover bus costs, costume expenses and choreographer fees.

PARENTS AS PARTNERS
Parents in our local community are efficient at the standard fund-raising events, managing the total undertaking from kick-

off to wrap-up. Having successfully raised funds through standard candy, pizza and poinsettia sales, the group decided to tackle something more monumental. When they decided to host a show choir invitational, everyone understood that the directors had neither the time nor the energy to tackle another project. For four years now, the parent group has managed an invitational almost entirely independent of the choral teaching staff. A coordinator assigns individuals to serve as committee chairmen. Each chairperson tackles one facet of the project (lighting, sound system, student food, decorations, hospitality, etc.) and manages it for a few years before training a new chairman. The rewards have been more than monetary. The invitational is excellent public relations for the community, drawing a substantial crowd of area residents. The positive response from participants generates a feeling of group pride, and the day-long event allows directors from around the state to share information and ideas. The parents have developed a tremendous feeling of pride in this project and have become fast friends in the process.

"If you don't believe in .cooperation, just observe what happens to a wagon when one wheel comes off."
—Unknown

While it may seem unreasonable to ask choir programs to fund themselves, just that is happening every day around the country. Most directors are fortunate that parent booster groups are willing to help in this capacity. It is necessary for directors to make the most of these volunteers, allowing groups the freedom to generate as many funds as possible.

A WORD OF THANKS

While most academic teachers require a clean room, desks, a chalkboard, books and materials, the choir director needs all that plus help with riser setup, concert scheduling, assistance in theater maintenance, transportation planning, clinician scheduling, contest management and more. One person cannot do it all alone, but in most schools help is available. The trick to maximizing the help available is in cultivating friendships. While it is sensible to be friendly to everyone on a regular basis, a few extra thoughtful words or deeds help to ingratiate oneself in important circles.

"The only difference between stumbling blocks and stepping stones is the way you use them."
—Unknown

A local administrator was flattered one spring to be invited to lunch by the choir department. The administrator in question was in charge of transportation and custodial staff, two departments absolutely critical in the operation of the choral music department. While the intentions that motivated the invitation were pure (the department was expressing appreciation for a successful year of cooperation and work), the department also had another project in mind where some resistance was anticipated. In the midst of a congenial lunch, the topic of some interior painting was broached. As expected, some opposition was encountered. The matter was not pursued, but again the department expressed appreciation for all the help received that year. Within one week the choir room wore a fresh coat of paint and file cabinets and doors were also refinished. Genuine appreciation shown in a variety of ways, whether it be a thank you note, a plate of cookies, a kind word or a lunch invitation serves the director well in making friends in important places, and thereby acquiring help from willing partners.

> *"Use what talents you possess; the woods would be very silent if no birds sang there but those who sang best."*
> —Unknown

STUDENTS AS PARTNERS

Because students have a vested interest in the choral program, their dedication is solid and they are predisposed to be active partners in the choral effort. There are numerous tasks that can be handled by capable students. Those with the inclination can be trained as leaders. Throughout the day, routine tasks such as attendance, folder distribution, and room setup can be assigned to choir members. Sharing the responsibility for such jobs not only relieves the director of mundane tasks, but benefits the students as well.

COMBINED EFFORTS

Sometimes one partner can be coupled with another to multiply the effects of the total effort. Students, parents and the community can be called upon to help. The music department was informed that future musical theater productions must be entirely self-supporting. The only funds to be spent were those which could be anticipated in revenue. With this severe restriction, major fund raising needed to be initiated. In addition to raising ticket prices, the department borrowed the idea of donors from a local professional organization. Through the efforts of students, the community was approached for support and donations. Student contacts netted in-kind donations for programs, posters, and tickets, but cash was needed as well, so in the printed program we published lists of donors identified as "Rave Reviews" ($1-$25), "Encore, Encore" ($26-$99) and "Standing Ovation" ($100 and more). Students in the musical were given donation sheets with instructions to bring in as many donations as possible. The response was impressive. From 60 cast members the production received five donors in the "Standing Ovation" category and 206 donors in the other price ranges. The page of donor names recognized the community for their support, and they along with the students who generated donations became true partners in this endeavor.

FACTS AND FIGURES

The business department is a logical partner when financial decisions and planning must occur. In most music departments money must be budgeted and responsibly managed for the areas of music purchase, travel, clinicians, and festival fees. Ignorance is not bliss when it comes to knowledge of the budget, including figures for each

> *"The mold of a man's fortune is in his own hands."*
> —Francis Bacon

account, how encumbrances are handled, and how records are kept. In music education, there is no "general manager" except the director in charge. The director cannot hide behind the excuse that he is an "artiste" and therefore too busy to think about figures and balances. A budget mishandled may conveniently disappear within a few years.

Sometimes one must firmly demand the proper tools needed to correctly manage a budget. A few years ago, after a change in business personnel, there was some disagreement over the details of the music budget. The office was requesting precise figures from the directors, without supplying balance sheets. Just as one would expect a monthly statement from a personal banker, the directors insisted on reviewing a monthly printout of the budget. With the proper information, the directors were able to work amiably with the business office. It is vital to become acquainted with the business office, and insist on the necessary materials needed to professionally manage a budget.

PARTNERS IN THE COMMUNITY

Consider drafting a letter each spring to the editor of the local newspaper. The letter can thank students' employers for their cooperation in helping singers hold jobs and still fulfill their music commitments. Thank individual businesses personally and credit managers by name. Saying a public thank you makes it more likely that students will find a cooperative attitude the next time choir activities require time off from jobs.

"Nothing stops the man who desires to achieve. Every obstacle is simply a course to develop his achievement muscle. It's a strengthening of his powers of accomplishment."
—Eric Butterworth

There are logical partners in the arts. Utilizing and developing liaisons with the audio-visual department, the art and humanities department and the band and orchestra department makes good sense. Any opportunity to affiliate should be exploited.

FRIENDS IN HIGH PLACES

In the local school, one of the most powerful partners is a principal or superintendent. Maybe (possibly!) he is just a great guy, a cultured fellow predisposed to support the arts. Maybe (probably!) it hasn't hurt that he always has a cake on "Bosses Day," an occasional award such as a "Friend of Music" plaque and a frequent thank you for his constant help. Such friendships are valuable and indispensable to all who pursue a quality choral program.

"Let us be what we are and speak what we think and in all things keep ourselves loyal to truth and the sacred professions of friendship."
—Henry Wadsworth Longfellow

SOME PRACTICAL SUGGESTIONS:

1. Make friends with the principal and stop in just to say hello. Keep him updated on choir activities so he feels part of the group activities and is never taken by surprise concerning choir functions.
2. Say "please" and "thank you" frequently. Those who become a partner in the choral endeavor are more willing to help again if the work is appreciated.
3. Bake cookies for custodians and other friends when they perform a job that is not part of the daily routine.
4. Form a parent booster group and allow them enough power and leverage to accomplish important goals.

5. Use student man-power and brain-power. High school students are capable, and often willing to undertake important responsibilities. Assign students to attendance duties, folder distribution, filing in the music library and answering the phone.
6. Some high school students are capable of running sectional rehearsals. Take advantage of their keyboard, vocal, and leadership skills.
7. Become acquainted with administrators. When they associate a real-life face with a request it will be more difficult to deny.

> *"A will finds a way."*
> —Orison Swett Marden

8. Get to know the secretaries, and make reasonable requests followed by sincere thanks and appreciation.
9. Engage community members in fund raising efforts by acknowledging donations publicly. Businesses can use the exposure as advertising and private citizens enjoy the recognition.

The job of choir director is too large for one person, but most directors are fortunate enough to have resources available. The successful program taps into whatever resources are at hand, and uses each available opportunity to adopt new partners in the search for choral excellence. In business the successful manager knows how to delegate tasks, and it can be the same in the school choral setting.

There is one word of caution to heed in this attempt to acquire assistance. No matter how much time, money or enthusiasm is lavished on the choir program by parents or others, the director must still make final decisions. Musical decisions regarding choice of music, performance opportunities, and concert programing are still the exclusive domain of the director. Work rendered should be appreciated and recognized, but must be treated as work freely volunteered with no obligation on the director's behalf to repay individuals through favors or undue power.

With a director firmly in control, and a willing band of volunteers from the ranks of students, parents, community and staff, the choral music program can reach remarkable heights of excellence and quality.

EPILOGUE: Evaluating Excellence

How does one define success? Or quality? Or excellence? Leonard Bernstein says the "measure of [an art's] success is the extent to which it invites you in and lets you breathe its strange, special air!" A choral program's success cannot be measured solely by the numbers enrolled, the audience applause, the prestige performance or the trophies garnered; however, these indications are often the reflection of a program that is successful enough to invite students in, invite parents in, and invite community members in "to breathe its strange, special air." While the specific measure of excellence is indefinable, the excitement excellence generates will be a magnet for all. While the definition of quality cannot be bound by exclusive parameters, an audience knows when something is good and will return for more. While success cannot be determined by scores or ratings, a community recognizes and supports a program that serves its young people well. Perhaps we cannot define success in words or numbers, but must rely on our intuitive judgment. How do we feel about what we are doing at the end of the day, and at the end of the year?

> *"Any great work of art is great because it creates a special world of its own. It revives and readapts time and space, and the measure of its success is the extent to which it invites you in and lets you breathe its strange, special air."*
> —Leonard Bernstein

As we are intuitive and artistic, so must we be practical and business minded. We cannot hide behind the "artiste" persona to avoid the mundane daily chores that are the building blocks of a successful program. We do more than direct our choirs. Our job description details work as recruiting director, public relations supervisor, morale booster, disciplinarian, counselor, research and development coordinator, artistic director, business manager, and community liaison. It is never enough to say, "I did my job and taught the music." It is our responsibility to insure that students learn and benefit from our knowledge and instruction, both musical and non-musical. If your initial reason for becoming a choral director had more to do with showcasing your own talents than developing the talents of your students, keep it a secret. You will certainly be found out if nurturing your own talent takes precedence over your students' progress.

It is our obligation to teach music, of course, but it is also our obligation to educate students in the art of becoming a person. Music education is a process by which human behavior is permanently altered and we play the exciting role of facilitator by providing the liaison between the music and the student. If we do our job well, students establish a life-long relationship with music. In this role of facilitator our goal must always be excellence. Whether we are preparing a song, or a person, the path to excellence must always be foremost in our minds.

If we find it difficult to evaluate excellence in a choral program, how do we evaluate the progress of a developing person? Ultimately, in any situation we each judge ourselves, and those who do it honestly look to outside sources for affirmation. Those who sincerely wish to improve, excel, and succeed compare themselves to the best, and strive to be on a par with the finest. The brave director endures criticism because he is forever striving to improve.

> "The quality of a person's life is in direct proportion to their commitment to excellence, regardless of their chosen field of endeavor."

The allure of an art so great that it "readapts time and space" and "invites you in" is the compelling force that drives us on in a quest for excellence.

It is our hope that those who teach music because they love it will create an art so powerful that everyone they touch will be drawn in to breathe its strange, special, air.

EXTRA! EXTRA!
A Collection of Inspirations

For many years we have collected short poems, newspaper clippings, Hallmark cards and short sayings culled from various sources. Not only are these used in our teaching but we offer them to our students to take into the world. Perhaps one day they will find need for these words of wisdom. Our collection of quotes has to do with living – with becoming a person of quality. We are happy to share our collection and apologize for not knowing the authors of many of them. Some are part of the public domain and have been handed down as folk songs are.

Resolutions for Anytime

- *Speak to people. There is nothing as nice as a cheerful word of greeting.*
- *Smile at people. It takes 72 muscles to frown, but only 14 to smile.*
- *Call people by name. The sweetest music to anyone's ear is the sound of his/her own name.*
- *Be friendly and helpful. If you would have a friend, be one.*
- *Be cordial. Speak and act as if anything you do is genuine pleasure.*
- *Be interested in people. You can like everybody if you try.*
- *Be generous with praise but always cautious with criticism.*
- *Be considerate of the feelings of others. It will be appreciated.*
- *Be thoughtful of the opinions of others. You are not always right.*
- *Be alert to give service. What counts most in life is what we do for others.*

It works well to establish a choral theme for each school year. One source of ideas can be the musical play that will be produced that year. For instance, when working on "Pippin" the theme could be, "We've got to be people who live all of their lives in superlatives." For "Man of La Mancha" the theme may be, "And the world will be better for this." Be creative! A theme can have any source, and any inspirational saying will do.

Inspirational phrases serve to renew the spirit and keep the flame burning. Keep such sayings inside your music folder as gentle reminders. When more than a gentle reminder is required, make a banner of one and hang it on a wall or wear it on your shirt.

Take Time for 12 Things . . .

1. *Take time to dream – it hitches your soul to the stars.*
2. *Take time to work – it is the price of success.*
3. *Take time to think – it is the source of power.*
4. *Take time to play – it is the secret of youth.*
5. *Take time to read – it is the foundation of knowledge.*
6. *Take time to worship – it is the highway of reverence and washes the dust of earth from your eyes.*
7. *Take time to help and enjoy friends – it is the source of happiness.*
8. *Take time to love – it is the one sacrament of life.*
9. *Take time to laugh – it helps with life's loads.*
10. *Take time for beauty – it is everywhere in nature.*
11. *Take time for health – it is the true treasure of life.*
12. *Take time to plan – it is the secret of being able to have time to take time for the first eleven things.*

Slow Me Down, Lord

Slow me down, Lord.
Ease the pounding of my heart by the quieting of my mind.
Steady my hurried pace with a vision of the eternal reach of time.
Give me, amid the confusion of the day, the calmness of the
*   everlasting hills.*
Break the tension of my nerves and muscles with the soothing music of
*   the singing streams that live in my memory.*
Help me to know the magical, restoring power of sleep.
Teach me the art of taking minute vacations – slowing down to look at
*   a flower, to chat with a friend, to pat a dog, to read a few lines from*
*   a good book.*
Slow me down, Lord, and inspire me to sink my roots deep into
*   the soil of life's enduring values that I may grow toward the*
*   stars of my greater destiny.*

—Ann Landers column (1992 Creators Syndicate)

Values

The greatest handicap – fear
The best day – today
Easiest thing to do – find fault
Most useless asset – pride
The greatest mistake – giving up
The greatest stumbling block – egotism
The greatest comfort – work well done
Most disagreeable person – the complainer
Worst bankruptcy – loss of enthusiasm
Best teacher – one who makes you want to learn
Greatest need – common sense
Meanest feeling – regret at another's success
Best gift – forgiveness
Greatest knowledge – God
Greatest thing in the world – Love

Suggestion: Put these values as a pin-up in your practice room.

Attitude
by Charles Swindoll

"The longer I live, the more I realize the impact of attitude on life. Attitude, to me, is more important than facts. It is more important than the past, than education, than money, than circumstances, than failures, than successes, than what other people think or say or do. It is more important than appearance, giftedness or skill. It will make or break a company... a church ... a home. The remarkable thing is we have a choice every day regarding the attitude we will embrace for that day. We cannot change our past ... we cannot change the fact that people will act in a certain way. We cannot change the inevitable. The only thing we can do is play on the one string we have, and that is our attitude ... I am convinced that life is 10% what happens to me and 90% how I react to it. And so it is with you ... we are in charge of our Attitudes."

Success

There is only one success . . .
to be able to spend your life in your own way.

—Christopher Morley

Secret Formula for Success

Success comes overnight to those who have been sacrificing,
slogging and searching for longer than they care to admit.

To be what we are, and to become what we are capable of
becoming – is the only end of life.

—Robert Louis Stevenson

It is in the process of enriching the lives of others
that our own life takes on meaning.

We can't all do great things.
We can only do small things with great love.

—James Kimmel

We're neither pure nor wise nor good.
We'll do the best we know.
We'll build our house and chop our wood.
And make our garden grow.

—Candide

We are all heroes,
you and me,
Everybody who faces the world as it is –
and sets out to be happy.

Man's clouded sun shall
brightly rise
And songs be heard,
instead of sighs.

—Godspell

Dignity is how you feel about yourself –
Not how you look to others.

Some people bring music to those whose lives they touch.

Success comes in cans – not in can'ts.

No rule for success will work if you don't.

Don't be content with being average.
Average is as close to the bottom as it is to the top.

The only place where success comes before work is in the dictionary.

Coming together is a beginning;
Keeping together is progress;
Working together is success.

The road to success is uphill – unless your father owns the company.

The surest way not to fail is to determine to succeed.

Nothing worthwhile is achieved without patience,
labor and disappointments.

Opportunity is often missed because we are broadcasting
when we should be receiving.

PERFORMANCE

Better to try and fail
Than to fail to try!

There is a kid inside all of us. Keeping the kid alive
is what performing is all about!

—dialogue from TV series "Fame"

The experience of music is a dialogue –
a conversation between the performer and the audience.

—dialogue from TV series "Fame"

Nothing great was ever achieved without enthusiasm.

—Ralph Waldo Emerson

Triumph requires both "try" and "oomph."

You can do anything if you have enthusiasm. Enthusiasm is the
yeast that makes your hopes rise to the stars. Enthusiasm is the sparkle
in your eyes, the swing in your gait, the grip of your hand, the irresistible
surge of will and energy to execute your ideas.
Enthusiasts are fighters. They have fortitude. They have staying
qualities. Enthusiasm is at the bottom of all progress. With it, there is
accomplishment. Without it, there are only alibis.

—Henry Ford

Winners Vs. Losers

THE WINNER
Is always a part of the answer;
THE LOSER
Is always a part of the problem.

THE WINNER
Always has a program;
THE LOSER
Always has an excuse.

THE WINNER
Says "Let me do it for you;"
THE LOSER
Sees a problem in every answer.

THE WINNER
Sees a green near every sand trap;
THE LOSER
Sees two or three sand traps near every green.

THE WINNER
Says "It may be difficult but it's possible;"
THE LOSER
Says "It may be possible but it's too difficult."

YOU HAVE A CHOICE:
  BE A WINNER

—Kaye Lillesand

Every choir functions as a team. Not only are the parallels between a fine choir and a great team remarkably similar but speaking in terms of team affiliates musical discipline with athletics, which holds great interest for young people.

Characteristics of an Effective Team

1. *Clear Purpose – The vision, mission, goal, or task of the team has been defined and is accepted by everyone. There is an action plan.*

2. *Informality – The climate tends to be informal, comfortable, and relaxed. There are no obvious tensions or signs of boredom.*

3. *Participation – There is much discussion and everyone is encouraged to participate.*

4. *Listening – The members use effective listening techniques such as questioning, paraphrasing, and summarizing to get out ideas.*

5. *Civilized Disagreement – There is disagreement, but the team is comfortable with this and shows no signs of avoiding, smoothing over, or suppressing conflict.*

6. *Consensus Decisions – For important decisions, the goal is substantial but not necessarily unanimous agreement through open discussion of everyone's ideas, avoidance of formal voting, or easy compromises.*

7. *Open Communication – Team members feel free to express their feelings on the tasks as well as on the group's operation. There are few hidden agendas. Communication takes place outside of meetings.*

8. *Clear Roles and Work Assignments – There are clear expectations about the roles played by each team member. When action is taken, clear assignments are made, accepted, and carried out. Work is fairly distributed among team members.*

9. *Shared Leadership – While the team has a formal leader, leadership functions shift from time to time depending upon the circumstances, the needs of the group, and the skills of the members. The formal leader models the appropriate behavior and helps establish positive norms.*

10. *External Relations – The team spends time developing key outside relationships, mobilizing resources, and building credibility with important players in other parts of the organization.*

11. *Style Diversity – The team has a broad spectrum of team-player types including members who emphasize attention to task, goal setting, focus on process, and questions about how the team is functioning.*

12. *Self-Assessment – Periodically, the team stops to examine how well it is functioning and what may be interfering with its effectiveness.*

What is Teamwork?

Teamwork is the ability to work together toward a common vision and the ability to direct individual accomplishment toward organizational (choir) objectives. It is the fuel that allows common people to attain uncommon results.

Teamwork is a challenge. It means coordinating our efforts with those of others, not solely for personal glory, but for team achievement.

Great discoveries and achievements invariably involve the cooperation of many minds.

The team player knows that it doesn't matter who gets the credit as long as the job gets done.

Effective Leadership

1. *Organized and able to delegate*
2. *Enthusiastic and empathetic*
3. *Informed and representative*
4. *Able to communicate*
5. *Visionary and able to see their part in the whole*
6. *Able to laugh, possessing a sense of humor*

"They say the whole is greater than the sum of the parts that it's made of" (*Pippin*). Here is the definition of some of those parts.

The Anatomy of an Organization

There are five major types of "bone" which form the basic anatomy of an organization.

1. *The Wish Bones – Members who wish the others would do all the work.*
2. *The Jaw Bones – Members who talk a lot but do little else.*
3. *The Knuckle Bones – Members who knock everything others try to do.*
4. *The Tail Bones – Members who always have something else to do at the last minute.*
5. *The Back Bones – Members who really work hard to get the job done.*

This untitled poem is a great reminder for singers to become actively involved choir members:

Are you an active member?
The kind who would be missed?
Or, are you just contented
That your name is on the list?

Do you attend the meetings?
And mingle with the flock
Or do you stay at home?
To criticize and knock?

When extra help is needed,
Will we be counting on you?
Or do you always find,
You have something else to do?

Are you an active member?
The kind who would be missed?
Or, are you just contented
That your name is on the list?

"That's Not My Job"

This is a story about four people named Everybody, Somebody, Anybody, and Nobody. There was an important job to be done and Everybody was sure that Somebody would do it. Anybody could have done it, but Nobody did it. Somebody got angry about that, because it was Everybody's job. Everybody thought Anybody could do it, but Nobody realized that Everybody wouldn't do it. It ended up that Everybody blamed Somebody when Nobody did what Anybody could have.

Initiative is doing the right thing without being told.

Forget your mistakes, but remember what they taught you.

He who stops being better stops being good.

The elevator to the top is out of order, you'll have to take the stairs.

Don't be afraid to go out on the limb – after all, that's where the fruit is.

Happiness is a byproduct of an effort to make someone else happy.

God loves you – whether you like it or not.

When your image of yourself becomes positive, so will your performance.

Don't find fault, find a remedy – anybody can complain.

You cannot hit a target you do not have.

You do not sing because you are happy, you are happy because you sing.

You never have a second chance to make a first impression.

No one has yet invented a successful substitute for work.

All people smile in the same language.

Don't be afraid of opposition –
remember, a kite rises against, not with the wind.

GREATNESS

We are selling greatness! We are selling great music and so we must be great conductors.

—Charlene Archibeque

A great conductor:
1. *has a sense of humor*
2. *has the ability to inspire*
3. *has superior knowledge of the material*
4. *has a love of music and kids*

We must preach the gospel of greatness. We must make our lives and their lives count.

—Charlene Archibeque

Howard Swan urges to remember the three H's
1. *Honesty*
2. *Humility*
3. *Humor*

Our students usually don't think our jokes are funny. A few years ago we made some small posters which we keep hidden behind the piano and the podium. If (when!) we say something funny, we hold up the "laugh" sign. We have an "applause" sign too. Below is a humorous piece about ways to drive our singers crazy and the companion piece about ways to irritate the conductor.

Ways to Irritate the Singer
By Eph Ehly

1. *Prepare singers' body and psyche then talk. (It's a trick teachers with discipline problems use – the only time to get attention.)*

2. *Get into the music then interrupt – stopping at awkward places. (Director not concerned with singers' gratification – insensitive to their mood.)*

3. *Say something like "follow the beat" then move about the room. (Insecure directors will walk too close to the front row.)*

4. *Insisting on precision but not showing it.*
   Insisting on precision but not giving directions.
   Criticizing singers before giving directions.
   (These directors try to elevate themselves into a position of superiority by being condescending.)

5. *Shout directions during the singing. (Ridiculous!)*

6. *Ask for pianissimo and show forte or vice versa.*

7. *Ask for energy but don't give any yourself.*

8. *Shshsh.*

9. *Clapping noisily every time you want to stop. Clapping beats. (Who needs to "feel" the beat – Singer or Conductor?)*

10. *Singing along. (Especially ugly when director is male singing with a delicate female part.)*

11. *Using four-letter words to be emphatic. (Don't offend anyone unnecessarily.) Four-letter words are 1) a sign of a weak vocabulary, 2) feeling insecure or, 3) wanting to be "cool."*

12. *Assuming that no one cares. No one is trying.*

13. *Expect them to do better without specific instructions. Making broad and general statements.*

14. *Picking at details while the ship is sinking. (To everything there is a season)*
   A time to mark phrasing
   A time to mark articulation/interpretation
   A time to work pitch and rhythm
   A time to mark mood and pace
   A time to mark poetry and personal involvement

15. *Shotgun approach. Giving directions on everything at once.*

16. *Giving directions out of order. (Voice/page, measure, beat, pitch and/or word.) Be consistent.*

17. *Standing too long or sitting too long. Insisting on singing posture too long. (A general disregard for all physical discomforts.)*

18. *Expect singers posture – neck and face without tension – but show the opposite. (Do as I say, not as I do.)*

19. *Never smile! Music is work, not fun! If you have nothing to critique you should not be on the podium.*

Be aware of diminishing returns!
A Good Rule: "WATCH ME, SING LIKE I CONDUCT!"

Ways to Irritate the Conductor

1. *Never be expressive (inform your face of what the song is about). (Consider the message of the text and personify.) "Happy Days Are Here Again-Expressivity."*

2. *Take a noisy breath. (Take a silent breath – rhythmic breathing) a silent breath is a good breath. Noisy breath has a constriction.*

3. *Never take more breath than you intend to use. Take only one real breath and that at the beginning of a song.*

4. *Let everyone see how hard it is to sing the end of a phrase without breath. (Hide your motor.)*

5. *Interrupt the line when you stagger breathe. (Leave out some notes, fade out-fade in.)*

6. *Heave the chest in a rise and fall motion as you inhale and exhale. (Keep chest comfortably high, expand and contract below it.)*

7. *Chew on the word, rushing to the diphthong. (Sustain the initial vowel sound.)*

8. *Form the vowel to about 1/2 of its potential shape. (Strive for well formed vowels. Consider: 1) how does it look, 2) how does it feel, and 3) how does it sound.)*

9. *Pretend your neighbor's vowel is a disease – stay away from it. (Strive for vowel uniformity.)*

10. *Be health conscious, avoid clear enunciation of consonants, especially fricatives. (The drama lies in the consonants.) (The rewards of exaggeration.)*

11. *If under 30 produce a tone quality at least 3-5 years younger than you are; if over 50 produce a tone 3-5 years older. (Natural, fee, vibrant) (Mature) (Sing your age.)*

12. *Don't be a "middle of the roader" either sing louder or softer than everyone else. (Relate dynamic levels to physical sensations.) (Cresc.-Dim. together.)*

13. *Vibrato vigorously either above or below the pitch so as to add additional overtones to the sound and to confuse the listener. (An uncontrolled vibrato has never been a pleasantry in an age – Donington.) (The degree of vibrato is related to the dynamic level.)*

14. *Sing from one note-to-the-next-note. (Sing from one note-THRU-the-next-note.)*

15. *When encountering a series of short notes, glide over them smoothly so as not to attract attention to their rhythm or their pitch. (Articulation)*

16. *The rest is written for the singer – not for the music. (The greatest tension can exist in silence.) (Emphasize the rest.)*

17. *Avoid dissonant music, it's unnatural and makes young people wild. (Develop skill in negotiating complex intervals and harmonies.)*

18. *Never tune a choir, this is a technique reserved for instrumentalists only. (Develop the inner-ear. Work with the mind and not the voice.)*

19. *Strive to be individual, be a non-conformist, be committed to your own interpretation. (Blend) (To blend is to create an Ensemble. All factors must blend, vowels, dynamics, timbre, accel., ritard, legato, staccato, etc. When minds think alike ensemble develops.)*

Quiz

1. *You are directing your choir and in the back of the room Johnny is being a nuisance. You let him get by with it until you realize he is eating a page of the music you are working on. Do you . . .*
   A. *Retrieve the page from his mouth with your baton?*
   B. *Pass out the* Seven Last Words of Christ *and make him eat six of them?*
   C. *Do nothing but smile because you know Johnny is going to be sick as a dog; the music he is eating has "copying is illegal" printed across it; we all know the printing ink is poison?*

2. *You've worked on a piece for weeks and the choir hasn't been able to tune some critical chords. Do you . . .*
   A. *Adjust the tuning by inserting your baton in the throats of your singers?*
   B. *Teach the choir the wrong notes and attribute the composition to Charles Ives?*
   C. *Tell your choir that they will join the ranks of the most elite choirs in the world if they can sing the chords in tune. They will achieve the rare goal of singing pitches as well as rhythms.*

3. *During a concert your star soprano faints and falls off the back of the risers . . . two bars before her big solo. Do you . . .*
   A. *Assist her back on the riser with the judicious aid of your baton?*
   B. *Do nothing because two quick thinking basses have ripped off her dress and put it on a tenor who sings it beautifully?*
   C. *Quickly decide to turn to the audience and sing it yourself. However, as you blast out the first note of the solo, your clever accompanist who also saw the soprano fall, skips the solo and plays where the choir comes back in, leaving you looking like a complete idiot?*

4. *You are having a parent conference in your office. A mother who had a brief theatrical encounter she refers to as a career, has just finished screaming at you because you didn't give her daughter Susie the lead in the musical. She accuses you of being prejudiced and says she is going to the Board of Education to have you fired. Do you . . .*
   A. *Hand her your baton and tell her to direct herself presto to the superintendent?*
   B. *Tell her you will put her darling as the lead next year when you do the musical, "The Monotone Angel?"*
   C. *Admit to the mother you made a big mistake. You couldn't understand why her daughter sang like a mule until today.*

5. *You are conducting a performance, coming up to a soft passage of music that you have worked on for two months. Just as the critical time comes, a baby cries in the auditorium and no one hears the soft passage. Do you . . .*
   A. *Silence the baby with a dart throw of your baton?*
   B. *Do nothing whatsoever because you discover it is the superintendent's baby and it can cry whenever it wants?*
   C. *Bring the baby up on stage and have your choir sing to it "Hush Little Baby" which you realize – as poorly as your choir sings – will either give the baby permanent loss of hearing or brain damage?*

6. *You have only one piece left at the end of your Christmas concert when your choir president steps out of the choir presenting you with a Christmas rose and your accompanist a $300 gold watch. Do you . . .*
   A. *Attach the rose on the end of your baton and decorate some internal part of your choir president's body?*
   B. *Turn to your choir and say, "Thank you for this beautiful rose which must have really set you back financially," then ask the accompanist if you can see her gold watch which you accidentally drop in the grand piano. As she reaches for it you drop the lid and crush both her hands. But, to show that you are in the Christmas spirit, you give her your rose?*
   C. *Recall that the band man called you out of class at least 10 times that month for the kids to raise money. Little did they know that during their absence you were going through their lockers confiscating their personal belongings which you sold – making more than $2000.*

7. *Your junior high class has decided – while you stepped out of the class for a minute – to be cute and bring the school mascot, Herbie the Hog, into the room. Herbie proceeds to wallow on your music and relieve himself. Do you . . .*
    A. *Stab the little porker with your baton?*
    B. *Mistake the hog for a certain alto and find it learns music faster, so you let it stay in the choir?*
    C. *Do nothing because you realize there are only two minutes left in the class and you're not using this classroom next hour . . . the band man is?*

8. *It is the last concert of the year and you are backstage ready to bring the choir on when Johnny tells you he needs to go to the bathroom. You tell him to forget it and proceed to usher the kids on stage. You realize you made the wrong decision when Johnny breaks wind right before the down-beat of Jester Hairston's "Hold On." Do you . . .*
    A. *Use your baton to plug the source of the disturbance?*
    B. *Try to make the choir think you didn't hear it even though it had a sound decaying time of ten seconds?*
    C. *Look at Johnny and ask him to give the starting pitch again?*

Now let's grade your test. If you answered all the questions "A," you need to go into the baton-making business. You'll make lots of money. If you answered all the questions "B," you need to do fewer Barry Manilow pieces. If you answered all the questions "C," then you are well on your way to being just crazy enough to be a successful and happy choral director. Of course you will die young, but with a smile on your face. If you answered neither "A," "B," or "C," but in their same spirit, it just might be that your students will sense the love of music you have in your heart and develop their own sense of joy.

All of us have experienced situations like those described above. At the time, they were serious, frustrating, and unpleasant – not giving us the laugh we might experience later, thinking back on them. If we could see immediate humor in many situations, we would get fewer ulcers, live through fewer hells, enjoy our work a lot more, give our students a greater opportunity to love what we love, and most certainly accomplish greater artistic results.

Many directors demean what they refer to as the cheer leading aspect of their work. I think it's something to be respected. I believe that choir directors should value and use cheer leading as an essential ingredient of successful teaching – motivating – accomplishing. It's an ingredient that can keep us young (as long as we don't lose our pom poms) and good. It can also keep us in touch with our students and can allow us to reach them in very important, life-directing ways.

I once had a doctor tell me that in my profession all I had to fear was not making music work. In his profession he had to fear not making life work. How wrong he was. How little he perceived the import of what we do. We guide and care for so much with our hands. We direct energy, emotions, spirits, consciences, cooperation, creativity, values, ethics, and beauty. No wonder we often take ourselves seriously . . . as we should. But, we shouldn't forget that seriousness can be portrayed in many different ways, and that humor is an important strategy in life. Seriousness, if all droll and somber, can be an obstacle to learning. As easily as that baby's cry destroyed the quiet phrase in the concert, you can destroy a student's love of music. On the other hand, the open expression of your love for life – often shown through humor – can create a student's love for music and for much, much more.

—Choral Journal

Ten Suggestions To Help You Become a Successful Teacher

1. *A friendly personality, emanating an assuring, pleasing smile toward all students, is the most important requisite to instill student trust and confidence in the teacher. This confidence becomes the basis of student motivation.*

2. *Recognize that all humans are different; consequently, treat each student as an important individual who has personal needs: dignity, recognition, challenges, and rewards.*

3. *Begin with positive recognition of student achievement, however slight it might be. Gradually motivate with constructive, helpful criticism in an explanatory manner.*

4. *Communicate to all students that you care and are concerned, not only for their progress in academic achievement, but, especially, in their total personal well-being. (This can be achieved without fanfare, many times through a gesture or a smile, or both; and it tends to be a strong motivating factor.)*

5. *Become as informed in your subject-matter as possible; always realize, and subtly convey this to students, that you can and do make mistakes. After all, you are not God, but human.*

6. *Whenever possible, relate the subject matter to the student's contemporary world; give him or her a feeling of the need-to-know in order to have a fulfilling experience and success in life.*

7. *As often as possible, utilize means and aids (audio-visual) that bring into play at least two of the five senses to help the learning process. This motivating and stimulating procedure leads the students toward greater clarity and faster problem-solving; and it causes students to focus on the teaching-learning act.*

8. *Be available, in fact, be mobile in the teaching act; utilize all of the teaching area. Avoid being glued to the podium; and seldom, if ever, utilize pure lecturing for other than explanatory purposes and limit it, if possible, to fifteen or twenty minutes.*

9. *Preparation is the key to confidence. In your lesson preparation, whenever possible, plan for a minimum of two different student activities relating to the specific subject-matter. This can be two or more hypotheses, approaches, chronological developments, causes and effects, etc.*

10. *In as many instances as possible, show your personal interest by your presence or participation in non-academic school or community activities. You will gain the students' and the parents' support and admiration; hence, they will have confidence in you as an interested and concerned person. Further, students will be motivated, personally and through parental interest, to follow you as a teacher in the classroom. Once you have the students' positive feeling toward you, your task as a teacher becomes more productive and personally fulfilling.*

Points to Ponder

After a while you learn the subtle difference
  between holding a hand and chaining a soul,
And you learn that love doesn't mean leaning
  and company doesn't mean security,
And you begin to learn that kisses aren't contracts
  and presents aren't promises,
And you begin to accept your defeats with your head up
  and your eyes open, with the grace of an adult,
  not the grief of a child,
And you learn to build all your roads today because
  tomorrow's ground is too uncertain for plans.
After a while you learn that even sunshine burns
  if you get too much.
So plant your own garden and decorate your own soul,
  instead of waiting for someone o bring you flowers.
And you learn that you really can endure . . . that you really
  are strong, and you really do have worth.

—Field Newspaper Syndicate
Ann Landers column

Trust in God, but lock your car.

Meet regularly with someone who holds vastly different views than you.

*Remember that what's right isn't always popular,
and what's popular isn't always right.*

When you feel terrific, notify your face.

*Remember that the best relationship is one where your love
for each other is greater than your need for each other.*

When there's a piano to be moved, don't reach for the stool.

*Hold your child's hand every chance you get.
The time will come all to soon when he or she won't let you.*

*Remember that everyone you meet is afraid of something,
loves something, and has lost something.*

Open your arms to change, but don't let go of your values.

*Think twice before accepting a job that requires you
to work in an office with no windows.*

"Go forth into the busy world and love it, interest yourself in its life, mingle kindly with its joys and sorrows, try what you can do for others rather than what you can make them do for you and you will know what it is to have friends."

—Ralph Waldo Emerson

The Meaning of Life

Relationship with others and
*   with one's own self.*
From what it is at birth
*   to whom we become as child,*
Adult, parent, grandparent and
*   ultimately, as ancestor.*
The meaning of life
*   flowers through relationship . . .*
Parenting, teaching, serving, creating,
Learning from nature, the sages, our peers,
From our emerging selves
*   in a state of becoming.*

—Jonas Salk

Class

Class never runs scared. It is sure-footed and confident. It can handle whatever comes along.

Class has a sense of humor. It knows that a good laugh is the best lubricant for oiling the machinery of human relations.

Class never makes excuses. It takes its lumps and learns from past mistakes. Class knows that good manners are nothing more than a series of petty sacrifices.

Class bespeaks an aristocracy that has nothing to do with money. Some extremely wealthy people have no class at all while others who are struggling to make ends meet are loaded with it.

Class is real. You can't fake it.

The person with class makes everyone feel comfortable because he is comfortable with himself.

If you have class, you've got it made. If you don't have class, no matter what else you have, it doesn't make any difference.

—Ann Landers column

We wrote these gentle reminders to ourselves. They are called "Great Expectations."

Great Expectations

1. *Our students need adult friendship but they don't need another contemporary. Be the adult in the student-teacher relationship.*

2. *Our students are people FIRST and singers second. Don't become confused. They are kids who sing and not the other way around.*

3. *Don't compromise. We want to make our students well-rounded contributors to society. Keep after them about good manners, appropriate language and inappropriate public display of affection.*

4. *Expect a lot from them. Don't underestimate what a high school student can do. And don't be a hypocrite. Remember that kids don't care what you know until they know you care.*

5. *We teach so much more than music. A well-read director who is informed about the latest in literature, art and world affairs brings a better perspective to his/her teaching. Don't neglect yourself. Most of us know a student for three and four years. We are obliged to give them as much as we can. Encourage life habits that are important such as leading a drug-free life, the habit of reading, and staying abreast of current events. A well-rounded person is more apt to enjoy a happy adult life.*

6. *Dress for success. Look like a professional if you wish to be treated like one. Remember that we are models for our kids on a full-time basis.*

7. *Don't roll over and play dead. If you want to build a fine choral program, you have to fight a few battles. You have to stand up for yourself and demand a share of the pie. Remember that you can't fix everything. Choose your cause carefully.*

8. *Be careful not to fall in love with your kids. They have the nasty habit of graduating and leaving you with a hole in your heart.*

Eph Ehly recites this poem often in his travels across America. It serves as affirmation to us all of the incredible power and importance of music in our lives.

For the common things of everyday
God gave man speech in a common way.

For the deeper things men think and feel
God gave the poet words to reveal.

But for the heights and depths that know no reach
God gave man music – the soul's own speech.

INDEX

BIOGRAPHIES

Nancy Smirl Jorgensen

Catherine Pfeiler and Nancy Smirl Jorgensen have taught at Arrowhead High School in Hartland, Wisconsin since 1984 where together they run a comprehensive choral program with an enrollment of over 400 students.

Besides their teaching responsibilities which include a musical, barbershop singing, a competitive show choir and vocal jazz ensemble, they also have presented sessions at the Wisconsin State Music Convention, have served on music selection committees for the state of Wisconsin, and have published articles in the *Choral Journal* and *Wisconsin Magazine*.

Under the authors' direction, the Arrowhead Concert Choir has appeared three times at the Wisconsin State Music Convention, performed with the Waukesha Symphony Orchestra, and appeared at the Carroll College Festival. The group has also performed at the Dorian Choral Invitational and has produced numerous recordings.

Both active in the local music community, Nancy performs with an early music ensemble and has served on the Board of Directors for Milwaukee's *Early Music Now*; Catherine performs in community musical theatre, most recently appearing in a production of *Evita* for the Milwaukee Players.

Catherine Pfeiler

Catherine earned her undergraduate degree from Mankato State University in Mankato, Minnesota and her Master of Music degree in choral conducting from Arizona State University. Nancy earned a Bachelor of Music degree from Alverno College in Milwaukee, Wisconsin and a Master of Music from the University of Wisconsin-Milwaukee.